Introducing John *In His Own Words*
Moriarty

Edited by Michael W. Higgins
& Seán Aherne

THE LILLIPUT PRESS
DUBLIN

First published 2019 by
THE LILLIPUT PRESS
62–63 Sitric Road,
Arbour Hill,
Dublin 7, Ireland.
www.lilliputpress.ie

Copyright © The Lilliput Press and the Estate of John Moriarty
Commentary © Michael W. Higgins and Seán Aherne

All rights reserved. No part of this publication
may be reproduced in any form or by any means
without the prior permission of the publisher.

A CIP record for this publication is available
from the British Library.

10 9 8 7 6 5 4 3 2 1

ISBN 978 1 84351 755 9

The Lilliput Press gratefully acknowledges the financial
support of the Arts Council/An Chomhairle Ealaíon.

Set in 12 pt on 16 pt Garamond by Marsha Swan
Printed in Kerry, Ireland, by Walsh Colour Print

Contents

An Introduction
  Michael W. Higgins — vii

Chronology
  Mary McGillicuddy — xxi

Storytelling and Personal Journey
  Michael W. Higgins — 3

The Mystical Voice
  Michael W. Higgins — 57

Walking Beautifully on the Earth
(John Moriarty's Relationship with Nature)
  Seán Aherne — 89

The Everlasting Hymn of Praise & God I Am
(John Moriarty and Sacred Ritual)
  Seán Aherne — 141

A Walkabout in Dreamtime Ireland
  Seán Aherne — 165

An Illumination: Coda
  Seán Aherne — 203

Notes — 207
John Moriarty Publications and Related Works — 208

An Introduction

Michael W. Higgins

I recognized him instantly. He is the model for the character John in Edna O'Brien's novel *The Little Red Chairs*. A friend of the New Age aficionado Fifi, John has been dead for several years but his presence is haunting, ubiquitous, paying regular visits via 'channelling' to the welcoming Fifi.

This John 'did rough work, digging and hoeing, quite content to do it since it kept him close to nature, and pursued his mystical studies at night … he would sit and talk at the kitchen table, expounding on God, paganism, Gaia, and St John of the Cross.'[1] He was a fount of exotic wisdom to the credulous Fifi, recording his insights – scribbles of mystical consequence – which she kept in a shoe box. Such scribbles consisted of: 'Let us return to the Bird Reign of Conaire Mor in which all things live Ecumenically with each other, man and beast uniting with nature in the grand scheme of things.'[2]

O'Brien never mentions John Moriarty but she draws the contours of his life with surgical finesse. But if he is an endearing and risible shaman in O'Brien's fiction, in real life he is anything but.

O'Brien's is the stuff of parody, of course, and she plays whimsically with a type of nature-loving, myth-dreaming, storyteller of forgotten truths in a plot that swirls with the sordid, churns up indignities the sane seek to deny, unearthing dangerous frauds who prey upon the credulous. It is a dark novel.

But I would never have recognized the caricature of Moriarty at all in O'Brien's novel had it not been for an Irish Christian Brother – variously a high-school teacher, chaplain, hermit, guide extraordinaire to all things Celtic in the south-west of Ireland – one Seán Aherne, a man overflowing with energy, curiosity and love of nature, a man who befriended John Moriarty, became his disciple and shared his wisdom.

On one occasion Seán asked if I would be interested in seeing where Moriarty lived and died at the foot of Mount Mangerton, County Kerry. I said yes, but more importantly, I wanted to know who he was – and the journey for me began.

Although the author of numerous books and countless audio recordings (he was a regular presence on RTÉ, Ireland's public broadcaster), he was not a paid-up member of the academy and remained an intellectual and spiritual outlier.

Brendan O'Donoghue, editor of *A Moriarty Reader: Preparing for Early Spring* (2013), remains convinced that 'Moriarty is very much underappreciated. I think that very few have managed to realize what he has achieved. My doctoral supervisor at University College Dublin compared him to Dostoevsky, claiming that like Dostoevsky he was not only not understood in his lifetime, he was not even misunderstood.'[3]

In part that neglect may have been attributable to the considerable popular success – national and international – of his immediate contemporary, the former priest, poet and Celtic spirituality superstar, John O'Donohue. The acclaim that accompanied O'Donohue's bestselling spiritual primer, *Anam Cara*, easily eclipsed Moriarty's more esoteric writings in terms of popularity and accessibility. They wrote at the same time; they wrote in the same region of Ireland; they wrote on similar subjects; they wrote with a poet's touch; and they died within months of each other.

Although O'Donohue's place in the Catholic pantheon remains secure, Moriarty is only beginning to come into his own. A more difficult writer who did not make compromises for his readers, who remained uninterested in celebrity status and who preferred a quiet, reclusive life over the perks of profile, Moriarty's especial genius is best captured by the Irish intellectual and public broadcaster Aidan Mathews:

> He may live in a caravan, a migrant among his settled readership, but he's not Sister Wendy whose toothy quaintness in a pantomime habit reassures a mass audience that spirituality is really rather charming, and he isn't Brother Ass either, awash with watercress

and Paternosters in the easy ecofeminism beloved of Sunday supplements. ... there is something magnificent about his single-minded oppositional stance in our deconsecrated world; and to watch him perform his rain-dance on the astro-turf is to witness an ecumenical invocation of all human spiritual authority, North, South, East, and West, against the power and dominion of technocratic consumerism, of the liberal laboratory outlook.[4]

Moriarty is Hibernian in his heart, his imagination, his sinews. His soul is one with the matter of Ireland.

But who is this peripatetic searcher, part academic, part gardener, part poet and part philosopher – a veritable bridge-builder among civilizations ancient and new?

He was born in Moyvane, County Kerry, in 1938 and received his secondary school education at St Michael's College, Listowel. While still an adolescent he made the first of many shattering discoveries when he realized that by reading Darwin's *The Origin of Species*, the story he lived in, the story that sheltered him, the overarching biblical narrative that he imbibed in church and school with its benign and uncritical fundamentalism, was no longer uncontested: 'It was my calamity that I had fallen out of my story. ... I had fallen out of a world into a universe that seemed infinitely indifferent, even hostile, to my purposes and yearnings. And the killingly lonely thing was, I didn't know of anyone else to whom this had happened.'[5]

Perhaps university would yield a new certainty the old consolations could no longer provide. He spoke to his father who at first was surprised by the request of his fourth child that he wanted not to settle on the land and buy a second farm but rather go to university. He asked John what he wanted to do and his son's answer was succinct and revelatory: 'It's a hunger that is in me.'⁶

This hunger was not to be sated, however, at University College Dublin, but rather ruthlessly intensified by the queries and probes unleashed by his reading of Kepler, Pascal, Coleridge, Melville, Arnold and Nietzsche – thinkers who in various ways underscored the common terror of humanity: the awe-inducing horror that we are barely awake in a universe unrestricted and expansive. Moriarty was not alone in his sickness, he now realized, but his own 'menacing inwardness' would lead him to distant ideas and distant places including, as Gerard Manly Hopkins would have it in one of his 'terrible sonnets' composed in a time of personal sundering and exile, 'cliffs of fall/Frightful, sheer, no-man fathomed'.

Adrift in London following his final university exams he became a vagrant, walking the streets and parks during the night, sleeping in a library during the day, living rough and unkempt. But he managed to secure a position as an assistant teacher of English at a Catholic boarding school for boys in Staffordshire. Still, it was more short term than expected. He succeeded in earning a premature termination following a parent's complaint to the headmaster.

Footloose once again. But not for long.

He telephoned one of England's foremost Catholic thinkers, James Munro Cameron, a convert from Marxism, a Balliol graduate, a distinguished essayist and occasional poet and head of the department of philosophy at Leeds University, who had earlier invited Moriarty to come to

Leeds to pursue a graduate degree in philosophy. He was disposed to take up the offer. Aware that Moriarty was penurious, Cameron offered him a job tutoring first-year students in order to ensure him some revenue.

While at Leeds Moriarty wrote that 'a lovely, lovely thing happened to me': he met Marilyn Valalik. They spent numerous hours walking together across the high moorlands of north Wales and during this time of intellectual and imaginative reverie he found himself unmoored to Descartes and enthralled by the logic and wisdom of *The Mabinogion*, a compilation of ancient Welsh wonder tales.

So enthralled, in fact, that he found himself increasingly drawn to literature as a source that could address the existential angst that continued to plague him. He boldly told his first-year philosophy students that 'for all its clarities, our Cartesian cogito is a cataract. In no way glaucous, wholly transparent, it blinds us to as much of what is out there as it lets in.'[7] It is time for a new epistemology, a time for new or fresh seeing.

And then Canada came calling.

Or, more precisely, Manitoba.

Serendipitously recruited by the mother of a student (she was an English professor on a lecture tour in Europe) to join the Department of English at the University of Manitoba in Winnipeg, he protested that his formation was in philosophy and that his 'academic credentials are quite forlorn. The only thing I have, which is a Bachelor of Arts degree, I didn't even go back to have conferred.'[8] But it didn't matter, this paucity of credentials. What mattered, and what clearly impressed the Canadian professor, was Moriarty's quick mind, effervescent wit, storytelling abilities and rebel's charm. It was, after all, the 1960s.

The ferocity of the hurricane-driven winds and waves that buffeted his transatlantic crossing prepared him for the fury of a prairie winter and reminded him of his need to experience nature, not simply to observe it. On one occasion, in an early March, he had his first taste of a prairie blizzard:

> My first impulse was to go out into the fields beyond the university and experience white-out. ... It was instantly and breathtakingly confusing. ... I realized that there was no way I could experience white-out and not die, and so, if only to salvage something of my self-esteem, I turned and faced into the blizzard as a buffalo would and I asked it to reave and bereave me of the old ideologies of domination. ... In this blizzard, it was somehow clear to me that we ourselves are the iceberg into which we will crash. Or no. Rather did it seem the case that we ourselves are the iceberg into which we have already crashed. At our very origin as a species, that's when we crashed.[9]

Winnipeg in the winter solidified his geological/poetical intuition that Darwin was right. It consolidated his view that, disengaged from our primal instincts, our companions in creation and our humble if noble birthing as a species, we are solely heirs to the constrictive reasoning of Bacon, Descartes, Newton and their Enlightenment spawn.

A true disciple of William Blake, Moriarty saw in the English mystic, painter and poet, a thinker and visionary who understood the dread consequences of a dehumanizing

Reason, the curse of Urizen or Single Vision: 'Blake is surely right when he insists that our modern, materialist cosmologies have their sources in the poverties and impoverishments of single vision.'[10]

It was in Canada that Moriarty would begin to tentatively unfold his new cartography of the mind and spirit. As he says: 'In Canada, for tundra reasons, it was with the most elementary forms of culture that I was happiest, and, among them, crying for a vision was as far as I could go. For some years now I was obsessed by the thought that Western Civilization had come to an end.'[11] Moriarty knew that he had to find a new way forward, he had to articulate a new way of living.

It was time to journey to the essence of our earth, recover the primordial mythology, the narrative of connection that had been sundered. He must seek his 'bush soul, my soul outside of society, my soul outside of civilization with all its restrictions and its Lady Windermere fans, my soul reunited with the terror and wonder of the natural world. And that, I clearly saw, meant returning to Ireland.'[12]

Queried as to what Canada meant for him, he responded with charity and insight: 'Like so many others, I came to the New World thinking of a future. That it gave me. But, as well, it gave me a past, an alternative to our European past, to go home with.'[13]

Returning to Ireland, keen on hearing anew the *vox hibernorum*, discovering afresh the spiritual temerity of the Celtic monks, he also found that the lure of the 'bush soul' was going to be more literal than metaphorical and that it had to be so visceral precisely in order for him to enter more deeply into the process of rebirth.

On one occasion, having freed a distraught swan caught in a sheep-wire fence, her four cygnets waiting on her release, Moriarty marvelled at their beauty and dignity. While walking back to his home, he 'skirted the small, almost dried-out marsh where her nest was. On impulse, I walked across and, lying down into it, I curled myself up as tightly as I could. In the end I was egg shaped, and I lay there a long time, acknowledging that I needed re-hatching, that I needed rebirth.'[14]

He was resolved that he 'would be the mosaic-maker of my own mind, and pristine sensations of the pristine world would be the tesserae'.[15] He would remake his own mind via his sensations and these would be by immersion – he would be utterly co-sympathetic with nature. He would need to slough off the encrustations of culture.

He found in Connemara the possibility of healing for those, like himself, 'disabled by the terrors of the new astronomy, the new anthropology and the new epistemology'.[16] He suffered from 'somatically sensuous deprivation. Lacking the sensuousness of sitting for hours under a waterfall, of walking in high heather, of climbing a hill, of listening to a sheep-farmer talking in Irish about winters past and to come.'[17]

Connemara was to be the antidote to Winnipeg's Urizenic tyranny. But Moriarty's comprehensive rejection of the consolations of the bourgeois world, his repudiation of the serene rhythms of ordered Western thought and his radical jettisoning of inherited religious 'truths' would exact a terrible cost. It wasn't going to be an easy rebirth. He would experience a dark night of the senses and a dark night of the soul, a levelling emotional void that would bring him to the cusp of disintegration. He 'broke down'.

The wholesale renunciation of his culture, creed and civilization, the no-holds-barred approach he took to his past formation, his total absorption into a new mode of being, commanded in the end a psychological and emotional cost of personally devastating dimensions: Walking down from the mountain near Loch Inagh it happened. 'In an instant I was ruined. Ruined beyond remedy and repair, I felt. The universe had vanished from round about me. I saw a last, fading flicker of it and then I was in an infinite void.'[18]

Swimming in a vortex of the self's unwinding, with little in the way of a still point, directionless and vacant, Moriarty somehow intuited in the heart of the maelstrom that he 'needed help in a way that I never before did. I fell instantly and instinctively *back* [my italics] into Christianity. Whatever else, Christianity was mother tongue.'[19] Undoubtedly, this wrenching experience was a potent mixture of the metaphysical, the psychoanalytic and the poetic. It was an emotional collapse or an acute clinical depression or a luminous insight accorded only the mystically inclined, or, most probably, a combination of all three. But it was indubitably a graced moment.

Moriarty conceded that up onto now he had 'played with the Christian myth,' but his transfiguration on the mountain shattered him 'into seeing. And it wasn't with my eyes that I saw it. It was with whatever was left of me that I saw it ... I was a Christian. Not a Christian again. I was a Christian for the first time.'[20]

Convinced that 'emerging from Gethsemane, Jesus left his curriculum-vitae face, his and ours, on Veronica's napkin',[21] Moriarty needed to craft a new theological narrative showing that Jesus lived a primordial truth, that it lived him and that his descent into the bowels of our geological history, of our material evolution, was an enfleshment too shocking to contemplate and too dangerous to ignore.

But if Moriarty was in intellectual turmoil and spiritual upheaval, his psyche was in meltdown. He suffered through dreams 'nightmaring' him without respite. He needed help and he found it on Boars' Hill, Oxford, in a Carmelite priory, with one Friar Norbert.

Moriarty 'told Norbert the whole story of what had been happening' to him, outlining what he graphically dubbed the 'dark, virulent infestation from within my own nature'. He was unsparing in his recollection:

> 'Is it madness?' I asked.
> 'No,' he said.
> 'Why do you not think so?'
> Quietly, he made a circle with his thumb and forefinger.
> 'In madness,' he said, 'the circle is closed. The person is engulfed, is often deluded and isn't able to distinguish what is really profound from what is trivial. In your case the circle is open,' he said, parting his fingers. 'You can walk round about your experiences and you make sense when you talk about them.'[22]

Although Moriarty could makes sense of his experiences, there was something as equally conceptual as intuitive going on; he was engaged in a larger task, a rethinking of dogma, a creative alignment of creation and redemption centred in the mystery and power of Tenebrae. John of the Cross, he argued, took Tenebrae seriously and so would he.

As traditionally re-enacted, Tenebrae involves a triangular stand with fourteen candles, each of which is extinguished following the serial chanting of the psalms of lamentation, until only the apex candle, the fifteenth, remains lit. Darkness penetrates; darkness encroaches; and then with the remaining candle taken below the altar or to a crypt, all is darkness.

Tenebrae defines the way of reconnection with our evolutionary path. This trail brings us to the earth's layers of evolution, to prehistoric times. This trail, a harrowing of hell less in Dantean and more in Darwinian terms, is pioneered by Jesus for all things, 'for stegosaurus and rhinoceros as well as for mollusc and Moses'.[23] Moriarty understands that this immersion in our geological past, this trail to the subterranean pulse of our species, must be reconfigured into ritual, 'into sacred things sacredly said, into sacred things sacredly done'.[24]

With a brazen creativity, Moriarty takes the original Tenebrae ritual and baptizes it anew: the ritual of our further and final evolution. Lamenting the fact that we have allowed our awareness of Christ in the Garden of Olives to eclipse our awareness of Christ in Gethsemane, our awareness of Christ on Calvary to eclipse our awareness of Christ on Golgotha, Moriarty argues with unnerving ingenuity that having crossed the Kedron, the Torrent,

Jesus goes forward in a double progress. In the first, setting out as Lamb of God, he goes forward through the Garden of Olives and Calvary, and, hell harrowed, he re-emerges in the Garden of the Sepulchre. In the second, seeking to pioneer the mystical way, not just for himself, but for all things, he goes forward as microcosm into Gethsemane, on to Golgotha, and, Ordovician desert dust in his hair, he comes back and, in all the world, there is neither bush nor star that isn't surprised by what has happened to it. In the second progress, occurring simultaneously with the first, Golgotha is the place of the skull, not also like Calvary, the place of a timber cross. It is the place not of physical but of mystical death, a dying so total that we are able in the end to say what Tauler said:

NON SUM.[25]

In his attempts to rewrite the Tenebrae ritual for a new age, Moriarty had no less an ambition than to unite the mythologies of the ancients, the theologies of diverse faiths, the histories of animate and inanimate matter, in a grand strategy of redress. To recognize that in reclaiming evolution as a divine trajectory and restoring 'the whole psyche for sanctity,'[26] Jesus redeems as he harrows.

This is not orthodox stuff and yet it has in it a deeply orthodox DNA. If Moriarty's heterodox reimagining of the Triduum Sacrum provides ample evidence of his conjoining of evolution with the Paschal Mystery, of his prophetic testing of the limits of doctrine and of reason, his reorientation of the sacral and the mundane is rooted in his 'Celticism'. If he was a scientist *manqué*, a mystic in the making, he remained always the storyteller, the modern bard deploying his love of orality with his philosophical insights, insights that were not drained of their vitality by the categories and discourse of the apparatchiks of the academy, blind to vision.

As the Canadian Catholic political philosopher Charles Taylor says in *The Language Animal: The Full Shape of the Human Linguistic Capacity*: 'It is through story that we find or devise ways of living bearably in time.'[27]

'Living bearably in time' in and through the telling of stories, the very making of the human narrative, is an activity touched by divinity. As Moriarty reminds his readers, 'it isn't only houses that shelter us. Only a great story can shelter us.'[28]

Although Moriarty needed to redefine, reimagine, re-appropriate this great story, he did so by digging deeper into the sacred caverns of prehistoric times and by exercising the bardic role of a new Patrick. He defined the state of religion in modern Ireland in stark terms; and he would have no truck with an ersatz Celtic spiritualism, an ahistorical love affair with a faux Celtic heart that makes light of the ancient myth dream and its authentic Christian soul.

That new Patrick is Moriarty. By the time he died in 2007 he had provided a new vision, a dreamtime – a creative commingling that seeks to bind in a fertile unity the immanent and the transcendent, the geological and the mystical, in a post-binary quest for a universal integration of matter and spirit, a pan-Christic labour that incorporates the wisdom traditions of all faiths. Nothing less than this.

This Celtic mode of perception, wedded to a theophanic grasp of the truth that is Jesus or Eternal Imagination, provides the substratum that runs through Moriarty's life: an epic visionary of Creation's ever-fecund unfolding.

Chronology

1903	Jimmy Moriarty, John's father, born 29 July in Baile an Lochaigh, Dingle, Co. Kerry.
1904	Mary O Brien, John's mother, born 16 January Barragougeen, Co. Kerry.
1929	Jimmy Moriarty and Mary O' Brien married in Springfield, Massachusetts.
1938	John Moriarty born 2 February in Moyvane, Co. Kerry.
1943–51	Attends national school in Moyvane.
1951–6	Attends St Michael's College, Listowel.
1956–8	Attends St Patrick's Teacher Training College, Drumcondra, Dublin.
1958–9	Teaches in Christian Brothers Primary School, Portarlington Co. Laois.
1959–62	Attends University College Dublin and graduates with First Class Honours in Philosophy and Logic.

1962–4	Lives in various locations between Moyvane and London with a spell teaching in a Catholic boarding school in Staffordshire.
1964–5	Tutors in the Department of Philosophy at Leeds University.
1965–71	Lectures at the University of Manitoba, Winnipeg, Canada.
1967	Summer rips to San Francisco, Mexico, Vera Cruz.
1968	Summer rips to London and Greece.
1968–9	Year off on half pay. Lives in France.
!969–70	Back in Canada, with trips to the Shetland Islands and London that summer.
1970–1	Final year in Canada. During the Christmas holidays he took a road trip from Manitoba through the Midwestern states to the Grand Canyon in Arizona.
1971	Quits his position in Canada and returns to Ireland in June; lives on the island of Inisbofin off the Connemara coast until September, then relocates to Ballyconneely on the mainland until 21 December, when he moves to one of Lynne Hill's cottages at Toombeola, near Roundstone, Co. Galway.
1972–4	Rents the cottage at Toombeola, living frugally, dependent on his savings from Canada.
1974	Begins work helping in the kitchen of Ballinahinch Castle Hotel in March and lives in the staff quarters there.

1974–6	Works and lives part-time in Ballinahinch, part-time at Toombeola.
1976	Spends a week in the Carmelite priory at Boar's Hill in Oxford and returns there for the summer from May to September.
1977	Spends the year at Boar's Hill, living with the monks and working in the gardens until he becomes ill and returned to Connemara in November.
1978	The early months of this year were spent at Toombeola recovering from illness, during which time he decides to seek work as a full-time gardener. Finds a position working for Robert Guinness at Lodge Park, Straffan, Co. Kildare.
1978–80	Works at Lodge Park until the sudden death of his mother, Mary Moriarty, in early January 1980. Returns to Moyvane and spends that year living at home with his father.
1981–2	Returns to Lodge Park and works there until the summer of 1982, after which he returns to Toombeola and begins working as a gardener on two local estates, Leitirdyfe and Lisnabrucka.
1983	Starts building a house on a site his neighbours, the McCahill family, give him.
1983–95	Spends this period in Connemara, living in his house at Toombeola, while gardening, writing and giving talks at various locations around the country. The Lilliput Press publishes *Dreamtime* in 1994.

1995	Moves to Coolies on Mangerton Mountain near Killarney, Co. Kerry.
1995–2007	Lives in Coolies while writing his Turtle trilogy, *Nostos, Invoking Ireland, Night Journey to Buddh Gaia, What the Curlew Said* and *Serious Sounds* (all by Lilliput) and his Slí na Fírinne publications. In 1997 he hosted a six-part television series, *The Blackbird and the Bell*, for RTÉ.
2007	John Moriarty dies on 1 June at his home in Coolies, Killarney, Co. Kerry.

Introducing John *In His Own Words*
Moriarty

Storytelling and Personal Journey

John Moriarty was a deeply autobiographical writer. He drew upon personal experience, anecdote, snippets and shards of memory, a vibrant and encyclopaedic deposit of stories, yarns, fables, myths, a veritable treasure trove of the fantastical and the inspiring, and wove all into a wide canvas of entertainment and edification. He was the consummate teacher and storyteller.

Whether regaling his readers/listeners – because he was the bard par excellence of post-Yeats Ireland – with stories about uncovering his 'bush soul', being transfixed by the void, discovering the sweet epiphany of love or exploring the deep resonance of the Fisher King myth for all ages and cultures, Moriarty knew the power of narrative, personal and communal.

One day, in a state that threatened to become perturbation, I cycled, not to Imleach dhá Rua, but all the way up to Loch Inagh. Leaving my bike, I crossed the plank bridge over the narrows between the two lakes and then I turned right, walking north along the forest road under the Bens. I had a tumbling mountain stream in mind and when I came to it I climbed and climbed, crossing from one to the other bank or making my way mid-stream, which meant rounding great boulders and clambering up over great bare obduracies of bedrock. Always when I came here I would sit in a little gorge that had in it a six-inch fall of water, a thing that would bring a lost humanity back to its paradisal senses. Quite simply, that underwater frieze of green, velvet mosses would compel you to re-estimate our galaxy. Today, however, I didn't linger here. Rough though the going was, I kept climbing, climbing, until something I saw stopped me short. Washed down I surmised by a flood and deposited on bare bedrock was the skinned, pink-fleshed foreleg of a lamb. What gave it its terrible, lurid pathos was the fact that it was left there in the shape of a Christian genuflection. Looking at it, I thought of something Paddy Joyce from Clenchoaghan on the other side of the mountains told me. Up here one day seeking to track down some sheep of his that had strayed, he came upon a berried holly bush and hung up right in the middle of it was the whitened skeleton of a goat. Clearly, seeing the rich pasturage of its leaves, the goat had climbed up into the bush, had hooked his horns on its boughs, and couldn't come back down.

The land and the goat.

The genuflection and the hanging.

The genuflection on a Gethsemane rock, the hanging from a Calvary tree.

It was like some awful re-telling of the Christian story. And so, far from Christianity being foreign to nature or, as Nietzsche might say, a poison and a pestilence to nature, it is, on the contrary, a living if still gruesome outgrowth of nature.

Anima naturaliter Christiana.
Mundus naturaliter Christianus.

Dispirited, I turned to come back and down, and then it happened. In an instant I was ruined. Ruined beyond remedy and repair, I felt. The universe had vanished from round about me. I saw a last, fading flicker of it and then

I was in an infinite void. And the terrible anguish was, not only was the world I had hitherto relied on for my sense of myself and illusion, it was a deception. In terms of the Hindu parable, the snake had vanished but I could not sense the rope. And I felt very badly done by. The way I had lived for the past three years, curling up in the swan's nest, healing my head in the hare's form, baptizing myself out of culture, practising being a standing stone, seeking to walk the earth with a barefoot heart and a barefoot brain – I felt that all of this was a genuine search for the truth, not a merely speakable truth, but a truth I would surrender to, a truth I would live, that would live me, not just for myself, but for others as well. And now, in an instant, it had all ended in ruination. The world in and through which I had been a self, that was an illusion, it had vanished, leaving that infinitely isolated self in peril of disintegration.

Trembling and bewildered, I got on my bike to come home. Coming down through Ballinafad, I thought it will be a good sign if the front gates are open. Since there was no one living in the front gate-lodge, Michael Vahey had locked and chained them at the beginning of winter. It gave me hope when, against all odds, they were wide open. I went down to Patsy and Bridie Prendergast. Patsy was the gardener and he and Bridie his wife lived in the gardener's house near the stables. Keeping it as simple as I could, I told them that something terrible had happened to me in the mountains. They did their best. Coming back through the garden in the small hours I thought it would be a good sign if my little clock had stopped at one thirty-one. Again, against all the odds, it had stopped, dead on one thirty-one. This was an old superstition of mine. Being the opposite or reverse of thirteen, thirty one was a lucky number, and there it was now, comforting me, giving me hope that I would come through.

For now, though, there was no relief.

Over the years, deliberately and of seeking set-purpose, I used to recite a Buddhist mantra:

Namo Amida Buddha
Namo Amida Buddha
Namo Amida Buddha

Buddhism is pleasant to look at, whereas, in its final redemptive moment, Christianity is horrible to look at. And yet, now that I needed help in a way I never before did, I fell instantly and instinctively back into Christianity. Whatever else, Christianity was mother tongue. It was to Christ and it was to the God that Christ called out to in dereliction – it was to both of them that I now called.

El Greco's *Christ in Gethsemane* came sensationally to mind, that melting red-robed Christ with the yellow angel hovering above him, offering him the chalice, a suffering that anyone, even Christ, would attempt to bargain himself out of.

I had, in some measure, suffered the desolations of the age: Kepler, Pascal, Coleridge, Melville, Nietzsche and Arnold

– to me these weren't just historical figures of external historical interest. On the contrary, they were stages of a progressive distress that I would sometimes be very badly afflicted by. But I coped. I didn't know that I could cope now. It is one thing to find oneself engulfed in an infinite universe that has neither centre nor circumference, it is something altogether for that universe to disappear, to vanish like a mirage, leaving you in the void. (*Nostos*, pp. 519–21)

*

I had asked Eileen if she'd like to go for a walk on her day off. It was a richly overcast day with a breeze strong enough to ruffle the surface of river and lake, the kind of day that a fly fisherman loves to open his curtains and look out at. And, sure enough, upstream from Ted's place, there was a fisherman reeling in a played-out salmon and big Tom Joyce was below at the edge of the water, his long-handled, hooped net at the ready.

We turned our attention to the stonechats flying in loud alarm among the furze bushes, warning their young to take cover. But then we heard a dull thud. The salmon was already lying in the heather and Tom Joyce was bent over crashing a blunt stone down onto his flat and, no doubt, bleeding forehead. In a week or so someone would lift a lid and there the steaming, garnished thing would be lying in a bright but not grail-bright tray on a table in Paris or

Cologne. The table would be covered with a starched cloth patterned throughout and at the edges with lovely lacework. The lighted candelabra would brighten the red wine. The silver service would sparkle, the jewellery would sparkle, the conversation also, and no one would hear the dull thud, thud, thud that we heard, the old stone-age thud heard no doubt fifteen thousand years ago by someone on the bank of the Dordogne, heard maybe by the very same man who painted the mural in the pit in Lascaux.

A sound from the time before the discovery of metal.

Going down the path to the eel weir, we crossed the bridge on to the island and then, unsteadily, we made it across the log bridge to the far bank. Keeping close to the river for a while, we ventured across the reed beds out into the wide open bogs beyond. Before long, the going uneven, we came to the first of a long string of lakes, called Arkeen Beg, that I had often come to seeking a particular kind of solitude. It had patches of dark shingle shore that had an iron ring to them. It had a small wooded island with a heronry. Today the herons were strangely silent, not even a single dispute over territory, not a single outraged movement from one to another roost. And as for the lake itself, a good salmon and sea-trout lake, two cormorants had it all to themselves. I looked intently at them and, as I half expected, one of them did look the worse for wear, quite bedraggled in fact. Only yesterday, crossing Tuaim Beola Bridge in the early morning, I heard a terrible alternately loud and muffled Mesozoic squawking. Looking over the parapet, I saw that it was an otter and a cormorant, he doing his vicious best to drag her down and she flailing him with her wings. Catching sight of me, the otter disengaged, dived and was gone, but the cormorant, poor thing, not seeming to know whether she was living or dead, she was just carried round and round, helplessly around, in the swirling current. So as not to further frighten her I held back. Eventually she became inelegantly airborne and headed up river, to this lake I guessed, and now again today, there she was, not so streamlined but, clearly, quite recovered from the shock and fright of it all.

On the way back downstream towards the river, we saw a water lily, fully open, its great green pads resting on black water. Drawn by it, we went close to the bank. Neither of us realizing that it was undermined, Eileen went right to the brink, it gave way and there she was sitting with the lily in its pool. Before I had time to take off my jacket and throw it to her as a lifeline, she had turned and was already clambering out. Back on her feet, she was still visibly frightened but of course she soon recovered and just laughed, looking back down into the caved-in world.

You're going to have to take them off and squeeze them, I said, looking at her dripping clothes.

Excusably, in the circumstances, I didn't offer to help. In a moment of unspoken understanding between us, I turned in all modesty and walked away, putting the eclipse of a hill between me and her.

A little incident, I thought, standing there. In outward appearance, a little incident but, in view of what I had been thinking for the past few days, full of portent.

Good portent, I felt.

Her world had given way under her, she had slipped into the dark water, but only to find herself at one height with hope, at one height with a gloriously opened water lily. In Hindu and Buddhist terms, at one height with a gloriously opened lotus. (*Nostos*, pp. 563–4)

*

One day weary from walking I lay down, flat-out, on a wave-worn bed of granite at the edge of a lake. In no time at all, and seemingly from nowhere, a scald crow circled, calling raucously. I knew what he was thinking, thinking with an empty craw, with an empty gut, mouth-wateringly, he was thinking that I might be carrion, so I lay dead-still, giving nothing away.

I knew the score.

An ewe is giving birth. Coming feet first, head first into the birth passage, her lamb has already developed rudimentary horns. For the sheer, tearing pain of it, it is a long and disabling parturition. Having spotted her in her distress, a scald crow is circling. Even if he tires of waiting and flies off, he will come back. Knowing when the stricken ewe is at her most helpless, he comes down and, they being exposed and open, they having no unchewable wool on them, he picks her eyes out and, blue in his beached bill, he flies off with them. Landing in what he considers a safe place, he drops them, he gobbles them.

The eyes with which I had seen the Parthenon.
The eyes with which I had seen the auroras of Chartres.
The eyes with which I had read *Romeo and Juliet*.
Those eyes gobbled.

Gobbled by a hooded crow for whom the Parthenon doesn't mean what it means to us, for whom Chartres doesn't mean what it means to us, for whom *Romeo and Juliet* doesn't mean what it means to us.

So this was it.

This was my bush soul.

My bush soul was being raucously overshadowed by the nihilism of Nature.

And the meaningless lap lap lap lap lap lap lap lap of it.

Disappointing the bird, I got up and walked. Neither from nor toward, my eyes not rightly seeing, I crossed into high heather. A hare sprang away from my feet and before I knew what was what I was on the ground and I was easing my head, face down, into the warm form. It was a perfect, sheltering fit and as I lay there, breathing in the rich warmth and the rich musk, I asked it to be two things: I asked it to be a poultice sucking out all that was damaging and limiting in my European way of seeing and knowing things and, that done, I asked it to be a cocoon bringing a new and blessed mind, a mind of Nature, to life in me. (*A Moriarty Reader: Preparing for Early Spring*, pp. 306–7)

*

Coming home after that first excursion in Greece I felt I could meet Newton and maybe hold my own with him. Newton had written a *Principia Mathematica*, but on the road south to the Labyrinth I had lived through a *Principia Mythica*. And from now on I wouldn't be bullied either by civilization or by science. From now on I would be my own man. Like a baron who had successfully contended with his king, I had come home with a mythic *Magna Carta*.

But now, the lake still mirroring the immaculate world and mirroring me in it, I had collided with what I had become, and I felt the anguish of having to start all over again.

I imagined it.

I would be the mosaic-maker of my own mind, and pristine sensations of the pristine world would be the tesserae. Taking my time with it, I would look at a patch of red sphagnum. Picking it from one of the wizened bushes behind me, I would taste a haw. Growing on the next rock I'd pass, I would touch a little tussock of sable moss. Without picking it, I would smell a stem of bell heather. And then, sitting by a turf fire at home, I'd listen to a curlew calling below on the shore. Starting again with sensations such as these, I'd remake my own mind.

On the way back across the bog I came to a stream that runs down into Loch Fada. Finding a place where the bank was level with the water, I knelt down and immersed my head three times, baptizing myself out of culture, baptizing myself out of Christianity. To complete the baptism, I knew I would have to come back a second time and a third time to do the same thing. It must be a baptism of thrice three immersions. Why, I couldn't consciously say. I was willing to accept that the whole psyche has its reasons. And I didn't wish to be impudently curious.

The girl at the check-out in Keogh's grocery shop wondered how I had contrived to look so like a drownded rat on such a dry day.

Instead of volunteering an explanation I sought to camouflage my embarrassment by doing what she so regularly did, I told her a joke.

'Why do ducks have webbed feet?' I asked.

'You tell me,' she demanded.

'For stamping out forest fires.'

'Why do elephants have big feet?' I continued.

This time, smiling broadly, she thought about it, but no …

'Well, aren't you going to tell me?' she asked.

'For stamping out blazing ducks.'

She laughed, but only obligingly, wondering if it was funny.

'You just wait,' she said.

'Wait for what?'

'You just wait till tomorrow evening.' […]

Here in mirroring Connemara maybe there is healing for everyone who has been disabled by the terrors of the new astronomy, the new anthropology and the new epistemology.' (*A Moriarty Reader: Preparing for Early Spring*, pp. 308–9)

*

I'll tell you a story:

In Africa, two or more centuries ago, a white man had accumulated a great store of precious, merchandisable goods. If only he could get them to Europe his fortune would be made. To further this purpose, he hired the best African porters he could find and one morning, having eaten, they assumed their burdens and set out, hoping to rendezvous with a ship that would be lying off the coast at the full of the third next moon. They weren't only strong men, these men he had hired. They were happy men. And, singing their ancestral songs as they walked, they were brave men. They didn't turn back, or so much as look back, at the borders of their tribal lands. Even in a seemingly endless savannah they were, happily, for going on. By the full of the second moon the white man was sure they would make it to the coast in time. Then one morning a strange thing happened. Strange, that is, to the white man. Sitting there, not eating, their eyes closed, the porters, to a man, sank into a trance. By midday that day, the man who must at all costs make his fortune was bullish. By midday three days later, he was totally at a loss. In the end, every ruse and remedy he could think of having failed, he sat beside one of them and, his bearing and tone altogether more accommodating, he asked him. Will you please tell me what is happening? Slowly, over hours, the porter came back from his trance. Yes, he said, I will tell you. During the past two and a half moons we have moved so far, so fast, that now, trance deep in ourselves yet awake, we must sit here and wait till our souls catch up.

That's the story.

In Europe during the past three centuries, we too have moved too far too fast. It is time, I believe, to do as the Africans did.

Among the first peoples of the world, loss of soul is thought of as the great illness. Only the most powerful shamans can deal with it.

Ever since Freud, however, the peoples of the West have talked and talked about suppressed sexuality, but have talked hardly at all about suppressed soul.

The question is: are we ill with the great illness? And, if not in our nature, are we, in our behaviour, aids virus to the earth? Are we doing to the earth what the aids virus does to the human body: are we breaking down its immune system? Is the earth HIV Positive? Is it HSS Positive? Homo sapiens sapiens positive?

I don't know.

Anyhow, that is one way of looking at this book. Disengaging from movement local, it invites us to give movement essential a chance.

And thereby hangs a tale, perhaps not a tale told by an idiot, but, reading your book, I was here and there aware of both sound and fury. So what, in this instance, does it signify?

Ironically, in view of what I've been saying, it signifies a voyage. A voyage, by movement essential, to where we are. And this voyage to where we are is, I believe, altogether more necessary for us than a voyage, by movement local, to the Moon or Mars. A giant step it would indeed be for humanity were someone to set foot on the earth, especially now that Darwin has shown how profoundly implicated in it we are. Relevant in this regard is an aspect of Nietzsche's discovery:

> I have discovered for myself that the old human and animal world, indeed the entire pre-history and past of all sentient being, works on, loves on, hates on, thinks on in me.

(*Turtle Was Gone a Long Time, Volume One: Crossing the Kedron*, p. x–xi)

*

There are three of us, a man, a woman, and myself. I am between them and we are walking back along the shore of the upper lake in Glendalough. We have been to St Kevin's cell and we have prayed there. Suddenly I'm aware that something acutely embarrassing is happening to me, a sword is falling out of my phallus. In pain and shame

I bend down seeking to retrieve it before it clangs, accusingly, on the hard, black tarmacadam path. But no, I don't succeed, and it clangs, it clangs, it clangs. Although they have observed what has happened, the man and the woman aren't at all surprised, or upset. I wake up. The next day I contact the woman and I tell her the dream. In prayer that evening, she sinks into a trance-like state. She is on the path by the upper lake. She comes upon the sword. Picking it up, she holds it, lying horizontally, in both of her hands, and she prays, asking the heavens that, they being gracious, it will never again afflict any man in the way that it afflicted me. As she stands there, holding it, praying, a ray of light reaches down from on high and, touching it, dissolves it.

Thinking of this dream and its sequel I have questions to ask: is there, if only in the form of unconscious celebration, a maimed Fisher King in every man? However palaeolithically pit-deep it might be, is there Fisher King trouble in every man? And what king of trouble is it? Did our forebears in medieval Europe misdiagnose it and did they as a consequence fail to heal themselves of it? (*Turtle Was Gone a Long Time, Volume One: Crossing the Kedron*, p. 22)

In the Waste Land everywhere there are stirrings of life. (*Turtle Was Gone a Long Time, Volume One: Crossing the Kedron*, p. 23)

*

And as for the myths that I've imported, I think of them as Magna Cartas, inspiring permitting and fostering a new way of being in the world, enabling us, for instance, to welcome the Lord of Life who, on a hot Sicilian day, comes to drink at our well. This surely is necessary among a people in whose cultural assumptions and axioms lie the seeds of ecological havoc. It wouldn't, I think, be altogether irresponsible to suggest that European culture must now run the risk of loosing its moorings to the ancient Mediterranean – to Hebrew prophecy, Greek philosophy and Roman law – in so far as we have thought of them as the normative perspective within which we have for so long attempted to organize ourselves and our world. I'm not talking about an exodus away from our past. (*Turtle Was Gone a Long Time, Volume Two: Horsehead Nebula Neighing*, p. xxxi)

*

My father was sitting under the mirror at the far side of the kitchen. Sometimes my father and his dog wouldn't only look at each other, they would seem to sit there conjuring each other across a limit of what was normally possible between an animal and a human being. That is what they were now doing, and I was happy to leave them to it, because for about ten hours a day, for the past three days, Darwin was guiding me into disaster. In a sense, the disaster occurred the moment I consented to walk with him. Since then, all I had done was to push on with him to the final enormity. It came when he led me in under a rockwall thirteen and three-quarters British Miles high:

It is hardly possible for me even to recall to the reader, who may not be a practical geologist, the facts leading the mind feebly to comprehend the lapse of time. He who can read Sir Charles Lyell's grand work on the *Principles of Geology*, which the future historian will recognize as having produced a revolution in natural science, yet does not admit how incomprehensibly vast have been the past periods of time, may at once close this volume. Not that it suffices to study the *Principles of Geology*, or to read special treatises by different observers on separate formations, and to mark how each author attempts to give an inadequate idea of the duration of each formation or even each stratum. A man must for years examine for himself great piles of superimposed strata, and watch the sea at work grinding down old rocks and making fresh sediment, before he can hope to comprehend anything of the lapse of time, the monuments of which we see around us.

It is good to wander along lines of sea-coast, when formed of moderately hard rocks, and mark the process of degradation. The tides in most cases reach the cliff only for a short time twice a day, and the waves eat into them only when they are charged with sand or pebbles; for there is reason to believe that pure water can effect little or nothing in wearing away rock. At last the base of a cliff is undermined, huge fragments fall down, and these remaining fixed, have to be worn away, atom by atom, until reduced in size they can be rolled about by the waves, and then are more quickly ground into pebbles, sand, or mud. But how often do we see along the bases of retreating cliffs rounded boulders, all thickly clothed by marine productions, showing how little they are abraded and how seldom they are rolled about! Moreover, if we follow for a few miles any line of rocky cliff, which is undergoing degradation, we find that it is only here and there, along a short length or round a promontory, that the cliffs are at the present time suffering. The appearance of the surface and the vegetation show that elsewhere years have elapsed since the waves washed their base.

He who most closely studies the action of the sea on our shores, will, I believe, be most deeply impressed with the slowness with which rocky coasts are worn away. The observations on this head by Hugh Miller, and by that excellent observer, Mr Smith of Jordan Hill, are most impressive. With the mind thus impressed, let anyone examine beds of conglomerate many thousand feet in thickness, which, though probably formed at a quicker rate than many other deposits, yet, from being formed of worn or rounded pebbles, each of which bears the stamp of time, are good to show slowly the mass has been accumulated. Let him remember Lyell's profound remark that the thickness and extent of sedimentary formation are the result and measure of the degradation which the earth's crust has elsewhere suffered. And what an amount of degradation is implied by the sedimentary deposits of many countries! Professor Ramsay has given me the maximum thickness, in most cases from actual measurements, in a few cases from estimate, of each formation in different parts of Great Britain, and this is the result:

	Feet
Palaeozoic Strata (not including igneous beds)	57,154
Secondary Strata	13, 190
Tertiary Strata	2240

– making altogether 72,584 feet; that is, very nearly thirteen three quarters and British Miles.

Led there by Darwin, I had come in under these sedimentary miles and I didn't know, looking up at them, that I would or could hold on to my mind.

It occurred to me that I should read the passage to my father, but looking across at him, I sensed that a gulf had opened between us.

I got up and went out into the yard. It was a wild night, the wind squalling from the west, and now, for the first time in my life, I found myself hanging in a kind of infinite isolation in infinite space, and there was nothing, nothing, nothing I could now, or ever, do about it.

Providentially, I believe, giving my mind something normal to be normal with, I saw a piece of paper being blown across the yard. Instinctively, I followed it, across the lawn, across the wall, across the road, and it was only when a twisting gust of wind lifted it and carried it up over the hedge into Welsh's field that I stopped, in one way stopped, because, years later, I was still following it in my mind, hoping that it would guide me past the lost God to a God I could once again believe in.

A few weeks later, meeting him on the stairs, the president of our college challenged me saying, 'You look so distraught these days, Moriarty. Is there anything you would like to come and talk to me about?'

I didn't tell him that, having crashed into Professor Ramsay's sums, my world, my biblical world, had gone to the bottom.

Nor did I talk to him about life in the new world, about life in the shadow of those infinitely indifferent, yet indefinitely damaging sedimentary miles.

It was in class, while we were revising a course in history, that I found what I at first thought was the perfect analogue to what had happened to me.

Christians and Aztecs had a different way of reckoning historical time.

In the Christian calendar, it was in 1519 AD that Cortez and his men began tumbling the world of Aztecs down the steps of its own high places.

In the Aztec calendar, this event took place in Year One Reed.

Year One Reed, clearly, was a frightful year for Aztecs. It was the year in which they lost their religion, their culture, their world.

Something like that has happened to me, I thought. I've undergone a Year One Reed.

Over and over and over again, now that I had lost it, I rehearsed it: I had grown up in a world which, according to Bishop Ussher's reckonings, the one true God had made in 4004 BC. It was a great drama, that world. A drama in five acts, the acts being Creation, Fall, Revelation, Redemption and Last Things. Having become incarnate in it, the God who created our world had left sacraments and commandments in it. By receiving the graces made available to us in these sacraments and by keeping these commandments, we could in the end win through to a life of glory. Alternatively, by rejecting the sacraments and breaking the commandments we could be running the risk of damnation. It was in other words a drama that had for issue one or the other of two stupendous possibilities, eternal bliss in heaven or eternal perdition in hell.

That was the story I lived in. That was the story that sheltered me. And now I knew that it isn't only houses that shelter us. Only a great story can shelter us. (*Nostos,* pp. 18–21)

*

Three days before Christmas I caught a bus to the Red Cow and from there I hitch-hiked home to North Kerry. Outside Loughhill, walking along by the Shannon, which was being carried back to Limerick by the incoming tide, a ramshackle car, a Morris Minor, drew up beside me. What I first noticed when I got in were the cold, perished hands at the wheel. Hands become stiff and awkward in their joints. Even as I talked to him, inevitably about the bad weather, my eyes kept coming back to them. Looking at them, an Elizabethan would say that they were the hands of a man of eighty winters, because a man of eighty winters is much older than a man of eighty years. A winter endured is wind endured and it is rain endured. It is a house whining at every sash, upstairs and downstairs, endured. For nights on end endured. Winter means a low, watery sun that doesn't come round, not once in three months, to the north gable of the house. A week of gales shaking its lichens off an old apple tree followed by a week of wind and rain, that would leave you having pity for bushes, that in itself would put ten years on a man's life.

There could be no doubt about it. I was sitting beside a man of eighty south-western winters. And it showed. In the creak, as of a creaking door, that his voice had become, it showed. It showed in the missing shirt buttons, leaving his chest as perished looking as his hands, a place of wispy whisperings whenever we turned a bend into the wind.

An old bachelor farmer if ever there was one, he was down now, he told me, to nine cows. 'How, with your hands as they are, do you milk nine cows?' I asked him.

'Whatever life is in me I get from the paps of cows,' he creaked. 'And do you know the grandest thing in the world? The grandest thing in the world is when you are teaching a calf to drink milk from a bucket. You must know what it is like yourself. You're Mororty, aren't you? I'd know you anywhere I met you from your mother. Ye had cows, so you must know what I'm talking about when you put your first two fingers into a calf's mouth and he curls his tongue round them, holding them tight against the ridged roof behind his moist nostrils and sucking them, drawing on them, like they were one of his mother's paps. That's when the life of the world comes into you, comes out into you from somewhere inside you, you drawing his mouth down into the milk, sinking your hand in it, so that he gets a taste of it. Three or four days later and he'll need no pap, but then another cow or maybe two cows will be calving and I'll tell you what you know yourself, being Mary O'Brien's son, a calf's tongue curled round a piece of old leather like me turns it back into short- horn hide, its fur licked into waves.'

He left me off in Tarbert and as I walked up the road, climbing the hill towards Tarmons, the Shannon a grandeur of water behind me, it occurred to me that an English sentence correctly translated into ancient Greek was what made the difference, separating my life from his life, separating my life from the life of my father and mother, she telling Gret Welsh that, what with my drainpipe trousers and long hair, I didn't even look like a fact of life.

But a calf's tongue curled round my first two fingers and therefore curled round a core of my being keeping its animal life alive in it – that indeed was a fact of life that I well remembered, and that was restored to me now, coming up to Christmas, by a man of eighty winters who, when he shook my hand with his perished hand, left the waves of licked cow's fur in it.

Coming to the top of Tarmons Hill I felt, as I so often did before, that I had come to a divide. Geographers talk of a physical, continental divide in North America. Mostly, it runs down along the spine of Rocky Mountains. On one side of this divide the rivers flow west into the Pacific. On the other side of it they flow east and then north to the Arctic Ocean or south to the Gulf of Mexico. For me, Tarmons was a spiritual divide. Behind me, the Shannon flowing through it, was a landscape that had in it a remembrance of Paradise. Ahead of me, the little tributaries of the Gayle flowing through it, was a landscape that had in it no very evident reminders of Paradise.

There are wuthering places, I thought. Places in which people and bushes and cattle are weathered, are wuthered, and this is one of them. All these fields, I could see, had been reclaimed or claimed for the first time from beneath the great raised bogs, only islands of which now remained. And a sense I had is that this land, rushy and wet, didn't want to be claimed, didn't want to be coerced into human intention and purpose. It was as though it resented its rebirth or its abortion back into daylight. And the best thing therefore to do with it would be to say a Requiem Mass on it, for it, and then, letting nature have its way with it, let a new raised bog overgrow it. As bog, with patches of bog myrtle, bog cotton and bog asphodel – as bog, with patches of sphagnum moss red and green – as bog, with patches of heather and sedge and dwarf gorse in it – as bog, with wild duck and curlew and snipe nesting in it and calling in it – as bog, this place I was born in and grew up in would remember Paradise, and it would give us images and metaphors for how we felt when we are in love. And then instead of me having to go and live next door to Lucy by Derwent Water I could ask Lucy to come and live next door to me. I could ask Lycidas to come, and in the lovely month of May there wouldn't be a snipe's nest or a curlew's nest or a wild duck's nest that we wouldn't know, and that way it would be about us and our place that Theocritus and Virgil and Tasso and Spenser and Sidney and Milton and Wordsworth would be singing.

But no. This wasn't Sicily in the Golden Age, and Amaryllis didn't live here, nor did Damoetas live here. This was where I grew up and Paddy Culhane lived here, and Mary Ann Danny O' lived here, and it was Mary Ann Danny O's eclogue that gave its own distinctive voice to the place:

> Isn't it a lonely place I am living in, and isn't it lonely I am myself looking out this door and seeing nothing coming towards me always but the blowin' wind and the wet rain.

Maag Mahony who lived in Poll agreed. Yes, Maag said, there are days when I look through my door too and the only thing I can say about the wind is that it is blowing and the only thing I can say about the rain is that it is wet.

North Kerry's eclogues.

North Kerry's antiphons.

A world, and it a wuthering world, coming to consciousness of itself. And yet, Mary Ann Danny O' was in all ways a more tremendous woman, a more tremendous being, a more tremendous Zoa, than Amaryllis would ever be. And she lived in a more tremendous world than Amaryllis lived in.

Of one thing I was sure. Neither Theocritus nor Milton had the measure, the literary measure, of Mary Ann Danny O', nor had either of them the measure of Poll, the few green fields aborted from the bog where Maag Mahony milked her cows, fed her hens and her horse, harnessed her ass and tackled him to her cart at around six o' clock, every morning, winter and summer, and then set out for the Creamery in Moyvane.

It occurred to me, walking a stretch of it now, that the road from Tarmons to Poll ran deeper into the world than the road from Athens to the Labyrinth did. Myths that walked with me on the road to the Labyrinth wouldn't, because they couldn't, walk with me on the road to Poll. I'd be altogether better able to sit in her house with Pasiphae than I would be to sit in her house with Maag.

Myth had encompassed Pasiphae, it hadn't encompassed Maag.

Myth had imagined Pasiphae to herself, it hadn't imagined Maag to herself.

Somewhere on the road to Poll, myth reached its limit and turned back on itself. Somewhere on the road to Poll, Western literature reached its limit and turned back on itself.

Somewhere on the road to Poll, the thread that Ariadne gave to our Western hero ran out and the golden bough no longer lighted his way.

Somewhere on the road to Poll, Jesus walked forward alone beyond those limits of daring reached but not overpassed by Herakles, Perseus and Theseus.

Whether Jesus made it all the way to Poll we do not know. What we do know is that on the road to Poll a saviour will soon find out what he is made of.

Maag Mahony, Mary Ann Danny O' and Mary Hegarty.

Seeking to imaginatively approach them, but not being so foolish as to think that I could imaginatively encompass them, I had often thought of them as North Kerry's three Sibyls, as North Kerry's three Norns, as North Kerry's three Fates, or best of all as North Kerry's three Graiai or Grey Ones. It would not surprise me if, in a dream of them, I saw that they had only one eye and one tooth between them and that these they would often pass back and forth between each other. (*Nostos,* pp. 147–50)

*

My father's Christianity didn't come to him through books or through sermons, yet when he talked, always in a few short sentences, about the crosses that come to people in life, or about life as purgatory, he left you with no response but silence. Arguments you could argue against, but how could you argue against a lifetime of experience, particularly when, in the experiencing, it interpreted itself, and did so independently of anything you could do about it?

It was strange to see them, my father and mother, getting on so well together.

It wasn't always so.

What was so strange is that when it came to listing and naming the great volcanoes in school, Vesuvius, Etna, Popocatepetl, Misti, Mount Helen – what was so strange is that no one ever mentioned our house.

It was a wonder and a terror when they fought. And knowing the danger, my father always kept his fare to London hidden somewhere in one of the outhouses and sometimes, there being no better remedy that he could think of, he would walk in the night to Listowel and, having not even a change of clothes, he'd board the early train to Limerick and Dublin. Within a couple of weeks we'd have a letter with his address and within a month Willie Door would come, all excited, down the road and in our gate with what we used call a wire – a wired cheque, that is. To see Willie coming was to know that money was coming. That evening we might have shop bread for supper.

Sitting by the fire now, I felt the perishing cold of a raw morning all over again. My mother, as she always did, came down to our room to wake us and tell us that Daddy was gone. Madeleine, my oldest sister, came in and taking me up into her arms she brought me out to the gable end of the house and we stayed there a long time in the first light of the morning thinking we might see the smoke of the train snaking its way from Listowel to Kilmorna.

And one night coming up to Christmas, when I was seven, Jim Guiney drove us all to Listowel and we stood on the platform, waiting, and we heard the whistles, three of them, and the noise, and then, its great lights almost blinding us, the thing that people called a train came in and no matter how big a fire we might have on at home, boiling mess for the pigs and the hens, our chimney never put up smoke and steam like that. The doors opened and standing in one of them was a man in a hat, in a blue double-breasted overcoat and with shoes so well polished you could see yourself in them, and that was him, that must be him, because my mother was going towards him, and while they were embracing I saw him looking at us and I wondered does he know which of us I am, does he know that I am John.

Ten years later, at the end of June, I was turning swaths of hay with a pike in the Hill Meadow, and I was fed up because it was a lot of work for one man and I wanted to be somewhere I might have a chance of seeing Bridie Sullivan. A car stopped at the gap. It turned and went away, and I saw a man who turned out to be my father coming towards me across the swaths, only six of them dealt with. Greeting each other, he calling me by my name, we shook hands. After a brief conversation, both of us needing I think to go apart and draw breath, he asked me if there was an extra pike anywhere. I told him where he'd find one, shoved into the briars inside the gap. By the time he came back, we were able for each other. We fell in working together, he, although he couldn't any longer be so sure that he was the master male, taking the lead.

I was sitting by a fire of loud, leaping excitements. The fragrances, separate and blent, of the burning, black turf and of the flaming, seething sticks could serve as incense, even as frankincense, for any altar, ancient Greek or Christian. But for all of that, it was only at odd moments that it claimed my attention, for I was thinking of that earlier Christmas Eve when I crossed the yard to the cowstall and crashed, mind and soul full on, not into a terrible something that was there, but into a terrible something that wasn't there. Standing in the door looking in, I was dumbstruck by what I didn't see, candles in the windows, holly and ivy hanging from the rafters and the tying posts. The radiance of angels I expected to see I didn't see, and as bad as all that was, the cows, some of them still on their feet eating hay, some of them lying down and chewing the cud, two of them turning to look at me – worst of all, none of our cows seemed to expect that kings would ride past the three doors of their house tonight.

It took me a long time before I could think it, but think it I had to: it was an ordinary night in the stall. It was only in our house that it was Christmas.

Coming back across the yard, I looked at the fowl-house and the piggery and it was the same story there. In both of them the same darkness and ordinariness as I had found in the cowstall.

That Santa brought me a game of Snakes and Ladders later that night didn't make up for this most killing Nativity out of things as I imagined them into things as they are.

Now, seventeen years later, a student of philosophy in University College Dublin, I could abstractly articulate what had happened to me. Standing in the door of the stall and seeing for the moment only what wasn't there, the word we fell asunder into *us-and-them*. From that night on, that new word, *us-and-them*, was a wound, open and gaping, that ran the whole length of our yard, separating animals and humans, and it was from the far, even far-off side of it that we now brought milk and eggs to our house.

Ours was a yard of two wounds: a wound heart deep to a pig and a wound heart deep to the word *we*.

As a lad I had held a basin to the gushing torrent from a pig's throat, but what basin could I hold to the wound in the word *we*?

What I was sure of tonight is that both wounds ended up as wounds in my mind and their bleeding there was fantastical not physical.

There was a question I would put to the Heavens.

If your Adeste isn't addressed to our cows as well as to us how can you expect us to be of Christmas good cheer on our side of the wound? If your Adeste, Venite and Videte aren't addressed to all things and not just to some things, how, once we've arrived in Bethlehem, do you think we will feel singing our exclusively human Adoremus? (*Nostos*, pp. 158–60)

*

By the time we were passing Land's End, tundra-bare but green on our right, it already looked like we might have a rough crossing.

By the time the mountains of south-west Kerry had sank below the horizon behind us the great dining-room was virtually empty at meal times.

By the time we overpassed the continental shelf and were heading out in the Pelagic furiosities of wind and water, there were ten or eleven of us who had the great lounge to ourselves. Among us were two Czech grand masters, so we spent a lot of time sitting at chess tables either playing or watching. Fortunately for me, there was someone as little skilled in the game as I was, so we had some great but of course wholly incompetent battles.

I would also go aside and sit alone.

I asked a sailor what the prospects for the remainder of the voyage were.

Unlikely that you'll be sunning yourself on a deck-chair, he said. It's a hurricane come up from below the Bermudas somewhere. It's blowing itself out right here in the North Atlantic.

In a way I was glad. I felt there was stuff in me that I needed to have shaken out of me. Recently I had begun to feel that if I could climb up into myself I'd come down looking as much like a chimney-sweep as I did coming out of a tree in a park in Leeds.

One day, yielding in the way that maybe King Lear would to a suggestion made to him by his Fool, I opened a storm-door and went out on deck. Momentarily, the screaming fury of the winds took my breath away but, seeing a pride of dolphins plunging along in what seemed like sheer delight beside us, I struggled forward and then downward by metal steps onto the lowest deck. Finding my way to the very bows, I bent over and greeted them, telling them that maybe one day dolphins and humans would drink to each other and to a common God from the kylix of Exekias. Coming back up the metal steps, I felt the plunge and, looking round, I saw a sea that had as much heaped up, overhanging water in it surely as was in the iceberg that sunk *the Titanic* and it fell, overwhelming everything, upon the very planks I had just walked back from.

Less than half a minute I realized, coming back in through the storm-door, had stood between me and being man-over-board.

The very thought of officials in Montreal checking their lists and finding that they were one short – that very thought cleansed me. It clarified me in my depths, taking from me a sense of existential composure that I never knew I had until I had lost it. Also, however few or many they might be, I felt that from now on all my days would be borrowed days.

That night, my sense of myself as a missing person not yet shaken off, I thought about the dolphins. It would have been defamation had I gone with the betrayals of language and called them a school of dolphins. It would have been defamation to have called them a pride of dolphins. And it wouldn't have worked at all to have called them a *thiasos* of dolphins. What I saw was a brightness of dolphins, a delight of dolphins, an amazement of dolphins.

What, I wondered, is their *Mabinogion*?

Suiting them so perfectly to their world, is their shape their *Mabinogion*?

Or is it that, being a wonder to themselves, they need no wonder-tales?

A sense I continued to have is that I had looked down upon ten or twelve *taliesins*, upon ten or twelve bright brows brightening the gloom of our Titanism.

In the end I was glad that I had opened the storm-door. I was glad that, looking down over the side of our Titanism in a hurricane, I had greeted them.

And the more I thought about it, the more I was convinced that the kylix of Exekias could be both image and icon of the new intelligence that Wallace Stevens had called for.

The dolphin-shaped boat that Dionysus reclines on, the boat whose sail is a spreading vine – more than the Parthenon, more than the Cnidian Venus, that boat is the primary revelation of the Greek world. And it isn't a revelation of or about a divine something behind the universe. It is a revelation of how the universe at some level is. In its presence, surely, the laws of gravity must make something less than the totalitarian claims that they currently do. A ship we have seen! A *Mayflower* we have seen! The *Mayflower* that will bring us to *Vita Nuova* in a *Mundus Novus* – looking into the universe with the eyes of Exekias, that we have seen!

What may flower did they have in mind? I wondered.

Could it be a flower that grew in our Hill Meadow?

Could it be the cowslip?

Looking into a cowslip one evening after school, I couldn't credit a Christian doctrine we had that day been further instructed in. In spite of the bad eggs or the bad meat that we'd find in our land, I couldn't believe that Paradise was lost to us.

I thought about Marilyn. Between games of chess and even during them I'd think about her. And always at night when I'd stretch out on a couch at the far end of the lounge in the hope that I might get some sleep there – then always I'd think of her.

This past summer we hadn't seen each other as often as we would have liked to. She was in Wales and I was in London, and in the end, after a long and bruising struggle, I hadn't asked her to come to Canada with me. To have done so would have meant that I was asking her to marry me, and I wasn't able for marriage, not now and maybe never, and the reason for this was as old as I was. I had spent the first eighteen years of my life inside of a marriage, the marriage of my father and mother, and I was carrying the damage of it in the deepest places of who I was. My oldest memory was of a fight, was of being wakened by it, and the killing thing in all of this was that my father was a good man, a very good man, an exceptional man, and my mother was a good woman, a very good woman, an exceptional woman, but you only had to put them together and there was trouble, sullen, silent trouble or loud, very loud trouble. Marriage for us was a blessing only when the Irish Sea flowed between the partners to it. By the time I was four I had decided that I wouldn't get married. I would live the way Jameen Kissane did and the way Dan Scanlon did. I'd have a few cows and a horse, above all I'd have a horse, and that way things would be as quiet as they were in Jameen's house, as they were in Dan's house. One evening when a fight was at its highest I went out and walked down through the haggart to McGrath's. Passing their kitchen window I heard them saying the rosary, and the contrast between the roaring in our house and the praying in a neighbour's house was saddening and shocking. And yet, even if I had the choice, I would choose my mother to be my mother and I would choose my father to be my father, only for God's sake don't have them within fighting distance of each other.

No. Eighteen years inside of a marriage, inside of a bad marriage, that was enough.

My father was a good man, my mother was a good woman, marriage was the culprit.

The culprit once, I wouldn't give it the chance to be the culprit again.

Like an electricity pole, marriage for me had the lightning sign, the danger sign, the sign saying, KEEP AWAY, on it.

William James likened a habit to a folded page that always wants to fall back on that fold. My attitude to marriage was a very old fold indeed, and it had been folded more tightly by every new row. Ironing out that fold wouldn't be easy. This time round, it got the better of me.

Also, there were needs in me that were bigger and, in the demands they made upon me and in the direction they were giving to my life, they were more totalitarian than my need for company and intimacy. They were needs that required solitude, more of it than I could ever legitimately expect to find within marriage.

In the end, I could only plead guilty to being the kind of man I was, and then go on and make the best of it.

So no, Marilyn. I didn't ask you to come to Canada with me, I didn't ask you to marry me, but you must have known that I wasn't just a wild-oats man, from beginning to end you must have known that my banner over you was love.

Fair sleep, she said, fair Fern Hill sleep.
Yes, I said, till you and I,
    till we meet …
        quite soon …
            in the Apple Towns.

From habit I suppose, even out here in this great waste or chaos of wind and water, I found myself thinking of a story told in yurts in the Old World, told in tipis in the New World: once upon a time there was a hunter who lived far off by himself in a part of the bush that was lonely even for owls and difficult for bears. Every morning at first light he would leave his hut and go off on a great round checking his snares and nets and traps, and looking for signs of animal movements in the night. Coming home one day, three trapped mink hanging from his belt, he saw smoke rising from his chimney. This was strange. In a world in which he never saw any human footprints but his own, it was very strange. All of his senses alert, he pushed open the door and now he saw that as well as a great fire on the hearth there was a steaming hot meal on the table. Signs of who might have done this there were none. Not on the floor, not on the walls, not on the wolf pelts that served him for bed clothes. Clearly, the meal could only be intended for him, so hanging up his bow and arrows and taking off the three mink, he sat down and he ate it.

Next morning at first light he was on his way. That evening, careful to stay downwind from a grizzly bear just out of hibernation, he turned for home and again, from a long way off, he saw smoke from his chimney. Pushing open the door, he saw a steaming hot meal on the table. On the third morning, his curiosity having got the better of him, he turned off his track and sitting concealed in a clump of bushes he kept his house in view. It wasn't long till he saw a fox trotting all the way to his door and pushing it open. Soon there was smoke, and so, instead of continuing on his round, he retraced his steps, closing the distance with all the patient, silent and invisible stealth of a great hunter. Entering the dark of his hut as noiselessly as his shadow would, he saw a woman bent over his fire, coaxing it into flame. Detecting it by its smell, he saw a fox pelt hanging from a peg on the back of his door.

Seeing him when she rose from her work, the woman said, I am your wife now. I will keep house for you. And if ever your hunting fails I will go with you into the bush. I will only need to sit on the ground and close my yellow eyes and then I will see where the animals are.

It was a new life for the hunter.

Every morning he had dry, well-mended clothes to put on.

Every evening, his belt laden or light, he'd see smoke in the distance.

Towards the beginning of spring, he complained of the smell of fox in the house.

Saying nothing, she carried on.

By the time the last great victory of geese had gone north, he was saying that he couldn't stand it.

One evening, his vexation intense, he sat as far off from her as he could.

Still saying nothing, she went to the door, she took down the fox pelt, she draped it over her shoulders and, turning back into a fox, she trotted away, never once looking back, into the bush.

A story about us human beings being able or not being able for the animals around us, I thought.

A story about us human beings being able or not being able for the animal in us, I thought.

How infinitely sad to see the animals giving up on us, to see the fox trotting away into the bush. (*Nostos*, pp. 199–202)

*

It was good to be back, living again on the bank of the Assiniboine, a river I still thought of as an upanishad flowing apophatically eastward into sunrise and morning across central Canada, a country whose name ends in *nada*, the mystical nada maybe, the *nada, nada, nada, nada, y en el monte nada* of the mystical ascent as St John of the Cross experienced and described it.

The silent river.

The apophatic river.

> He must know somethin
> He don't say nothin.

Most certainly, though, he does something. Something extraordinary. Joining the Red, he allows himself to be converted by it and together they go north into the white rigours, into the white *rigor mortis*, or into the white *rigor vitae*, of an Arctic winter.

Rivers flowing north to Hudson Bay.

Rivers flowing south to the Gulf of Mexico.

The Saskatchewan, the Assiniboine and the Red flow north and even when they are snowblind in winter I imagined that they somehow mirror me, that they clairvoyantly mirror me, mirror me awake and thinking, mirror me asleep and dreaming. Shaped as it was to stasimon and Psalm, they one night carried my mind north through taiga and tundra, and it was there in Nature's *nada*, in a sense it was there that I completed the poem I had last worked on in San Francisco. In it, a destitute Classical-Christian world has heard and heeded the call of Odysseus, not as Homer imagined him in Achaean times, but as Eva Gore-Booth imagines him in modern times, a mystic sailing north past Greenland into a greater world of greater Gods:

No drawbridge came down for Tristan, Iseult;
No drawbridge comes down
Yet lovers exult
And Daphne has crossed
The cold Danube, the Rhine:
When Daphne takes root
At the northern tree-line
She bears the red fruit of lovers although
Her boughs are stigmata under the snow.
Yet if she, like trees, taking root can outgrow
The desire to be always in leaf,
When the ice-age grips the fire's last coal
She will bloom like a rose tree
About the north pole.
Hell is filled with fire and ice,
Terza rima thunders fill Paradise,
And for three weeks during Fall
When the landscape gives the apocalypse
A final curtain call,
Beatrice too is a tree of our time:
Having roots in the circles of crime,
Such fire from the earth as she retrieves
Shows in the rose tree's laureate leaves:
Having hanged drawn quartered many an hour,
The rose will pull down the last church tower.

Insurgently, the piece takes on a double hegemony, the cosmic hegemony of the second law of thermodynamics and the cultural hegemony of the peoples of the ancient

Mediterranean, of peoples mirrored by the Tigris, the Euphrates, the Nile, the Jordan, the Ilissus and the Tiber, not by the Yukon, the Saskatchewan, the Assiniboine and the Red.

It is in espousing hylozoism that the piece takes on the second law. The word *hylozoism* is a compound of two Greek words, of *hyle* meaning matter and of *zoe* meaning life. Etymologically, therefore, the word declares that matter is alive, alive in mountains, alive in seemingly dead planets, alive in stars. Although not biologically alive in them, it is alive in rocks. Although not biologically alive in them, it is alive in thunder and lightning. And how right, how in accordance with reality, Native Americans are when they think of thunder as Thunderbird. According to the Oglala, Thunderbird lives on a western mountain. Sometimes she flies eastwards over the Rockies and when she does the flashings of her eyes are lightnings and the flapping of her wings are thunders.

I would think of Wolf Collar in his Blue Thunder tipi.

Now and then I'd imagine Newton and Descartes sitting either side of him.

Getting up, Wolf Collar draws a zig-zag line on the ground from the fire to the door. Coming back, he sits down and then a flash of blue lightning runs along the line.

As William James learned, there should be no premature closing of our account with reality. As Haldane knew, the universe is queerer than we can even imagine. (*Nostos*, pp. 312–13)

*

In January Winnipeg was a refrigerated city, colder, much, much colder than it was in the freezer of my fridge. After all, the freezer of my fridge didn't have a thin, stripping, forty mile an hour polar wind blowing through it. Days there were when Winnipeg did, and on days such as these it wasn't exactly a delight to see your bus pulling away while you were still a hundred yards off.

Continuously from December on, Winnipeg was a city besieged. Besieged not just at its perimeter. It was inwardly besieged. Besieged in every house and room. Rare were the days therefore when Tweedledum and Tweedledee would make much headway seeking to persuade us that the cold that besieged us wasn't really real. In Winnipeg in winter, for the most part at least, Dr Johnson got things ignorantly and brutishly right. And to prove the reality of reality in Winnipeg in winter, you didn't have to kick it. It kicked you. And there was a cat in the grin. And the cat in the grin had claws, he had teeth. Push your luck with him and you found out how suddenly and ferociously he snarled.

One day I did push my luck. Paul Vincent was a student in one of my classes and I had come with him to spend the weekend in a cottage owned by his parents on the shore of Lake Winnipeg.

Late in the afternoon on Saturday, Paul went into the kitchen to prepare the vegetables for dinner. By that time I'd had enough of reading, talking and listening to music, so I went to the porch, put on my winter gear, which made me look as wide as a bear, and I went out.

So white was the snow under the pines that it was a sacrilege, a sacrilege of purity against ordinariness, against the ordinary world. In the ordinary world we can be altogether less than perfect and in conscience we can get away with it. But here, no. Here, walking out onto the brilliantly white, wide lake, I for the first time recognized that as well as a sacrilege of sin there is a sacrilege of purity, and it seemed to me that of the two the sacrilege of purity is the more culpable. But out I walked. Rough going though it was inshore, I kept going and then suddenly so level was it that I no longer had to pick my steps, now I could walk it blindly, and I did, out, out, out into the sacrilege, into the purity. Looked at from the shore I knew that I would now be a shimmer, but I kept going, as a shimmer I kept going. No longer visible, from the shore not visible, I kept going,

North

north

north

Out where maybe an angel wouldn't go

Out where maybe an archangel wouldn't go

north

north

north

letting this sacrilege of purity take hold of me totally

almost totally

That evening I felt that only very little of me had come back.

I said nothing to Paul, or, when I returned to Winnipeg, to anyone else. But it took days and days and days before I recovered my common instincts for the common world. (*Nostos*, pp. 322–3)

*

It always delighted me to wake up on a Monday morning and think, today I'll be working in Lisnabrucka. As well as Lisnabrucka itself there was the road to it. Already by Ted's place I'd be in sight of the river and on a morning when it was in flood it would be tearing along in its rocky side channels and, while it would be silent and sumptuous in its main flowing, it would, overall, be severally and variously loud. And it wasn't only the river that flowed. A reminder of the vast tectonic pressures they had been subjected to when they were still miles deep in the crust of the Earth, there were patterns of lovely slow flowings in the crystalline rocks. And if there was an Atlantic gale blowing directly upstream the river would seem to be standing contrariously still. And no image of itself this morning in the river beneath it, a heron flying downstream into that gale would eventually give up and veer away so perfectly that not even a single tail feather or wing feather would be ruffled. And how different all of this from how things would be on a calm summer morning. From weather being the chief all-contesting, all-whelming reality now again the hills and the heathers and the rocks would come into their own. A salmon would leap and if he had gone grey I'd know that he had been quite a while in the river. If on the other hand he was a flash of shining, silver brightness I'd know that he had only recently come in, probably in the last tide, and it might be that he was headed upriver, up into Ballynahinch Lake, through a narrows in it called Snabeg, on into the river narrows between this lake and Derryclare Lake, round Derryclare Mountain, into another quite turbulent river narrows between Derryclare Lake and Loch Inagh and all the way through to the gravels at the mirroring far end of it where he was spawned. Here, as throughout, Loch Inagh mirrors the Bens and the Maam Turks, and you'd wonder whether these mirrorings didn't continue to brighten his mind in the deeper and more sullen feeding ground off Greenland.

And what for us is the equivalent of a salmon coming into his home river?

What for us is the equivalent of a salmon leaping out of his element?

Some mornings I'd see a heron fishing in a quiet water, out of the flow, under the far bank, and it wouldn't surprise me if he suddenly emerged from his heron-shape and walked towards me as the druid he was in an earlier incarnation.

Whatever else, I must remain alert to the surprise of things. Even now, in a reed bed downriver, it could be that a grub who has lived in the mud underwater is emerging into a dragonfly. And, almost certainly, somewhere on Derradda

Hill there is a caterpillar, already prestigious in colour and form, who will one day turn into an emperor moth, and who can say that the four false eyes on his wings upper and lower are in fact false? And could it be that I am cycling to work in a universe that has already spun a cocoon for itself and, if so, what, that is now unimaginable, will it emerge into? Or, having utter confidence in it, will I resign myself into it saying, Now this morning, here in Connemara, I turn my mountain bike into whatever metamorphic direction it has taken?

As with the part so with the whole.

As with the emperor caterpillar so with the universe.

A salmon, just in from the sea, leaping out of its element and, not so bound as we had thought, the universe leaping out of the atoms it is transiently composed of. Leaping out of them or leaping metamorphically out with them, neither it nor they what they hitherto had been.

For years after I first encountered it, the second law of thermodynamics violated me. Whenever I thought unrelentingly about it, it reaved and be-reaved me of self-significance and self-worth. Taking my cue from two French books, I was but a briefly enduring instance *of l'Homme Machine* caught up in *Mecanique Celeste*. A thinking machine in an unthinking vast machine, both machines meaningless, both doomed. The question was, how could such a sense of myself not debilitate me in my instinct for life? How pathetic our feelings! How pathetic Petrarch's sonnets to Laura, Dante's sonnets about Beatrice! How pathetic our regenerative dance about our regenerative maypole on May morning! How pathetic Nietzsche's tragic sense of life? Macbeth was surely right, life 'is a tale/Told by an idiot, full of sound and fury,/Signifying nothing.' And the nothing it signifies is nihil. The nihil of nihilism. Some nights the thing to do was to go home alone. But all of this changed when I came to Connemara, especially when I came to live beside the Owenmore. Until I came upon something like it within myself, the Owenmore was soul to me. In Hindu terms, as well as being sushumna to the land it was sushumna to me. Even on a grey day its pools were chakras and, grey morning or bright morning, cycling to work I would be mirrored in three of them. Looking down into them, I'd think, in them I see everything that modern science doesn't wish to see. I'd look at the water and think, it isn't only what it is composed of, two atoms of hydrogen and one of oxygen. I'd look at the mountains and I'd think, matter is mind in hibernation. I'd look up into the night sky and I'd think, yes, Albert, space-time is curved: like the Buddha on the night of his enlightenment it is sitting in the lotus position.

The heart has its reasons, Paschal says. And the naked eye also: alchemically and therefore philosophically sublimed by what it sees here in Connemara, it is entitled to its conclusions, all of them set down together constituting the new Philosopher's Stone.

Not itself a particular isolated thing, the Philosopher's Stone is a way of seeing no matter what particular thing, a cow dung or a star.

Here in Connemara, it was first of all in my senses not in my sub-psychic depths that I found my soul. I saw it flowing over an impediment of stones set down across this river, the purpose being to back the water up into a long pool so that salmon and sea trout could still ascend even after weeks of dry weather.

Coming upon it among the Elgin Marbles in the British Museum, I had seen diaphanous silk windrowed over a striding divine thigh. No question, it was a miracle, and yet, for pure, suave sensuousness, it was a poor thing compared to water flowing over this other divine thigh of ordinary local stones sunk into the bed of the Owenmore. If, walking this way, she saw it, Aphrodite must surely experience a need, an aching aesthetic need, to worship something divinely higher than herself. If, walking this way, he stopped to look at it, Socrates must surely experience a need, an aching, aesthetic need, to re-estimate the relative worth of sense and intellect, of sense and soul, the consequence being that all of subsequent Western history would be unrecognizably other than it has been.

This marvel of marvellously flowing and falling water taught me sensation. In giving me perception uncontaminated by conception, it gave me a soul, and for me it was a blessing as big as redemption, as big as salvation, that I passed it every Monday morning cycling to work in Lisnabrucka. (*What the Curlew Said*, pp. 65–8)

*

Invitations to give talks here and there throughout the country continued to come, but recently I had been backing off, telling people that I was played out, shagged. I sensed that the mysterious weakness that had flattened me some years ago was now again coming down over me and coming up over me. Then, before I had time to properly adjust to the idea, it was clear that my time in Connemara had come to an end. Seamus O'Brien, who had been building a house for me in Kerry, phoned to tell me that, while it wasn't finished, it was habitable. Next day word came through from the Lake Hotel on the shore of Loch Leine in Killarney, that they were looking forward to seeing me take up work as their gardener there. As it happened, Pat Crowley, a friend of mine from West Cork, had come to stay with me for a few days and so it was that, having packed some things in his van one morning, we were on the way south.

Things turned out as I feared they might. Cycling home from work that first evening I had to get off and walk to the top of the first low hill. That's how it was on every hill. And then came the steep and winding climb inside the road gate. Reaching the top I rested and, needing to hear it as well as say it, I said, Things aren't getting any easier.

By midday on Friday I was holding on to a bough of a lawn tree. When I was able I went into the hotel and phoned Fr Pat Moore to come and take me home.

Three days later I got a letter from Marie Hughes in

Dublin asking if I would come up and go over some texts with Martin who was soon due to sit his BA degree finals in English and history. She took a first, a second and a third long look at me in Heuston Station and she decided that she was taking me to see a doctor.

His guess was that I had ME or Chronic Fatigue Syndrome.

I came home five days later resigned to sit it out. So here I was, living in a new house, among mountains that were new to me, with my immediate neighbours, the Brosnans, not knowing what to make of me, but willing, with welcome in their eyes, to give me the benefit of the doubt.

This flourishing weakness, which a second doctor diagnosed as burnout, didn't come as a surprise to me. I worked in three big gardens/grounds and, in each of them each day, work had to be a big day's work. I gave talks and sequences of talks around the country and this meant that I had to keep coming up with new themes, new topics, some of them a real risk and difficult and burdensome to deal with in public. I'd sit and write almost every evening and that meant standing on dangerous ground or on no ground at all in one or another of the deep places within my own psyche, a common consequence being that I was often quite spooked as I climbed the stairs to bed. I spent more time than was good for me down among the sea floors of the Karmic Canyon. Every time I went back down I hoped it would be the last but it never was. So intense sometimes was the strain that I'd think, just as a lung can collapse so can my psyche. (*What the Curlew Said*, pp. 285–6)

The Mystical Voice

Moriarty was not a professional academician; he was not a theologian; and his training in philosophy – formal, that is – ended with an undergraduate degree in the discipline from University College Dublin. But he was a deeply learned man, possessed of a Promethean intelligence, formidable memory and a capacity for prodigious reading. His interests were eclectic, wide-ranging, and fuelled by a relentless intellectual and spiritual curiosity.

If he was part ecologist, part environmentalist, part folklorist and part historian, he was withal a profoundly religious thinker. And his religious thinking and spiritual nature were fed by the myths and theologies of world religions, dead and thriving, fed by the archaic wisdom of the extirpated cultures and elders no longer with us, fed by the living traditions of the diverse faiths that make up the human species.

Although pan-Christian in many ways, an unorthodox visionary who eschewed dogmatic certainties, who revelled in the extraterritoriality of fresh and new thinking, Moriarty knew the sacred texts of the Hindus, the Buddhists, the Muslims and so many others, but it was to his own story, out of which he had fallen and which for many years he sought to reclaim, the Christian story, that was the cantus firmus *of his questing heart and mind.*

How else can we find our way into that first, spinning morning?

How else can we find our way out on to the fields of praise?

Blake is right.

Haldane is right.

Dylan Thomas is right. (*A Moriarty Reader: Preparing for Early Spring*, p. 304)

*

Unlike D.H. Lawrence, I believe that the venture hasn't gone out of Christianity. But this is not a reason for complacency. As I see it, it isn't only the Christian churches that are in trouble. Christianity as a story is in trouble. It is in trouble in its images and in its metaphors. And, even though it ravages me to say so, it is, I fear, in trouble in its central ritual, the Eucharist.

If we do not get the diagnosis right, it is unlikely that we will happen upon the right remedy.

Christ who continues to grow and outgrow among us is the remedy. That and our willingness to grow and outgrow with him. (*Slí na Fírinne*, Preface)

*

Of someone who has died we say in Irish, *tá sé, tá sí, imithe ar shlí na fírinne*, meaning that he, that she, has set out on the path or the trail of truth. In Irish, the idea is numinous with a sense of final adventure, the adventure of our immortality. This is lost in translation, so it is best to stay with *Slí na Fírinne*. (*Slí na Fírinne*, p. 1)

*

Towards the end of July I had lunch with Babs, my sister in London. She worked as an air hostess with British United Airways. Looking at the books I had bought that morning, all of them books about ancient civilizations, she told me she could get me a cheap flight to somewhere within easy reach of one or another of them. I had no problems choosing which one, and that evening she phoned me to tell me that she had booked a return flight, open at both ends, to Athens, with a stopover in Rome on the way back.

Three mornings later, seeing it in a moment of delighted but frightened surprise, there it was, this pillared – what? this pillared thing – this pillared declaration – declaring what? Declaring itself forever untroubled, forever untouched by human turmoil – there it was, the heavens themselves declaring that relations between them and everything beneath them would never be anything but serene.

hadn't anticipated anything of this. Sight of it, sight of the Parthenon in the high distance, was a blow to me. I took it on the chest and, as though I was the dresser at home in Ireland, it shook all of classical learning out of me, it shook a kind of secular impiety out of me.

It wasn't that I saw it as threateningly holy, but the moment I saw it I did feel that I was down here and it was up there. More than anything else, I sensed its high, ontological apartness and this evoked or begot – as if from the place where the divine 'Thou shalt' came down upon Jews, it begot a feeling of reverence in me – that, and a need for contrition. I had come here in lordly mood but now if I was anything I was a pilgrim, paying tribute.

And as well as this, there was the pure aesthetic shock of it. The uncomplaining, confident, calm regularity of it. In the midst of all the surrounding irregularity, the very bold regularity of it. Very bold it certainly was, but was it also a little indecent I wondered? Indecent in that it made no concessions at all to how things are with us mortals. Could I trust anything that would so banish all disorder and confusion from my mind? And yet I only had to look at it to lose the argument. And not only that. For the first time in my life, however late in the day, I wanted to enlist with Greeks going off to fight at Marathon, going off to hold the pass at Thermopylae. There is, I thought, a citadel that must be defended.

Having seen this thing, this pillared declaration, I felt I could now turn round and go back to the airport and go home. (*Nostos,* pp. 60–1)

*

And then there was St Brigit, an early, exemplary saint these monks would have private and communal devotion to.

It was because she was a wonder-worker and, in that, showed the power of the new God in her, that she was exemplary

In Brigit's time it happened that a big, lustful man wanted to have his way with a girl, a maiden, who was thinking of taking the veil. To further his purpose, he gave her a silver brooch, asking her to keep it safe for him. A few nights later he contrived to steal it and he threw it into the sea. Going next day to the girl, he asked to have it back. Since, as he well knows, she doesn't have it to give, he puts it to her that either she has it for him by the following evening or she goes home with him. In her distress, the girl goes to St Brigit. As they are talking a man comes with a fish for the saint. When they open it, they find the brooch inside.

A man with a sack full of something on his back passed Brigit on the road one day. 'What's in your sack?' Brigit asked. 'Stones,' the man said. 'So it will be,' Brigit said and so it was. Weighed down and distressed, the man came past her again. 'What's in your sack? Brigit asked. 'Salt,' the man said. 'That it will be,' Brigit said. And, happy now, his load lighter, the man continued on his way.

Seeing that Brigit was weary with long travelling, an old woman of Brega invited her into her house. Having nothing else by way of food, the old woman killed her only calf and having nothing else by way of firewood she burned her weaving-beam. Next morning the calf was in her haggart and the weaving-beam was on her floor.

One day Brigit was herding sheep in the plains of Kildare. It rained torrentially. When it stopped she took off her cloak and hung it on a sunbeam.

These, and other stories about St Brigit, the monks who lived in this abbey would have known. And they also would have known about Ciarán of Saighir. On the night she conceived him, Ciarán's mother dreamed that a star came from heaven and entered her mouth. A wise woman herself, she didn't need to ask anyone, *file* or druid, what this meant. Of a heavenly disposition since the day he was born, Ciarán grew in grace and at the age of thirty, desiring to be ordained a priest, he went to Rome. After a few years there, he met St Patrick, who gave him a bell, telling him to go back to Ireland and to build a monastery wherever the bell rang three times of its own accord. It rang at Saighir, and that's where Ciarán started clearing the ground. He was helped by a wild boar, a badger, a wolf and a fox. And these, when the monastery was built, became his first monks.

They'd have heard of Colman Ela, a saint related in blood to a dynasty of famous high kings. Two babies, only days old, were given into Colman's care. In innocent, unembarrassed response he grew two breasts:

> Two paps has Colman Ela
> A pap of milk, a pap of honey –
> His right pap for fair Baithín
> And his other pap for Ultan

Of a famous hermit they'd have heard. Though living alone, he wasn't entirely solitary, for he had a cock, and, after a few years, he found himself befriended by a mouse and a fly. Crowing every morning, the cock would wake him for matins. If ever he fell asleep during one of his long night vigils the mouse would nibble his toe and wake him, and to help him as he read the Psalms and the Gospels in a fading light, the fly would walk back and forth beneath every line.

And they'd have heard of Kevin in Glendalough. Not easy on himself, Kevin used to pray in the *crosfigil* posture, in the posture that is of Christ on the cross. His cell being as small as it was, this meant that his hands protruded through two little windows on either side. One year a blackbird built her nest in his right hand. Reciting Psalms continually, Kevin remained as he was till the eggs were hatched and the nestlings had flown.

From all of which I would draw a simple conclusion.

When, in our world, the temperature drops below freezing point, very surprising things happen. Water, even where it is fluent or turbulent, turns to ice. Instead of rain we get snow. In damp houses, frost flowers bloom on the window panes. The moisture in our breath condenses in the air before us.

But, as there is freezing point in the world, so is there a miracling point. People, usually people who meditate and pray, come unexpectedly into it. In the end they live from it, and then they don't even need to perform miracles, miracles simply happen in their presence.

After years on Tai-shan, one of the four sacred mountains of China, a *wu-wei* sage comes back down to his village. As he walks past it, a dead tree blooms.

A universe in which a caterpillar becomes a butterfly might itself one day spin a cocoon, leaving us having to think again about our dogmas, religious and scientific.

The Silver Branch
and
A cloak hanging on a sunbeam

Surely, whoever reckons with the universe must reckon with these.

A cosmology that doesn't reckon with these is reckoning with something much less than the whole story.

The whole story requires new eyes, new mind, new intelligence. It requires new lives.

On the way home, this time the impulse not so compelling, I crossed the fields and lay down in the swan's nest.

After about an hour it felt like a raft, and it was carrying me over nine waves to Ireland. (*Nostos,* pp. 434–5)

*

Next morning I went out into the woodshed and with an axe and with wedges and a seven-pound sledge hammer I spent the whole day splitting two trailer-loads of timber that Michael Vahey had left in. Split logs for the fires, for the fire in the big lounge, for the fire in the study and for the fire in the bar, they to me were what rivets were to Marlow, a kind of amnesia, an anaesthetic which, if it didn't quite quench my mind, did what I hoped it would do, it beneficently narrowed it.

That evening I sat in what for me was psychically safer ground, thinking of cultural implications. To begin with the cultural implications of two propositions, one, that with Christ we have come off the detour that has been Western history since its beginnings, the other, that with Christ we are back on the evolutionary trail.

Blake would build a northern Jerusalem:

And did those feet in ancient time,
Walk upon Englands mountains green:
And was the holy Lamb of God,
On Englands pleasant pastures seen!

And did the Countenance Divine,
Shine forth up on our clouded hills?
And was Jerusalem builded here,
Among these dark Satanic Mills?

Bring me my Bow of burning gold:
Bring me my Arrows of desire:
Bring me my Spear: o clouds unfold!
Bring me my Chariot of fire!

I will not cease from Mental Fight,
Nor shall my Sword sleep in my hand:
Till we have built Jerusalem,
In Englands green & pleasant Land.

Hostile to Jerusalem and Christ, Shelley imagined another Athens:

The world's great age begins anew,
The Golden years return,
The earth doth like a snake renew
Her winter weeds outworn:
Heaven smiles, and faiths and empires gleam.
Like wrecks of a dissolving dream.

A brighter Hellas rears its mountains
From waves serener far;
A new Peneus rolls his fountains
Against the morning star.
Where fairer Tempest bloom, there sleep
Young Cyclads on a sunnier deep.

A loftier Argo cleaves the main,
Fraught with a later prize;
Another Orpheus sings again,
And loves and weeps and dies;
A new Ulysses leaves once more
Calypso for his native shore.

O, write no more the tale of Troy,
If earth death's scroll must be!
Nor mix with Lain rage the joy
Which dawns upon the free;
Although a subtler Sphinx renew
Riddles of death Thebes never knew.

Another Athens shall arise,
And to remoter time
Bequeath, like sunset to the skies,
The splendour of its prime;
And leave, if nought so bright may live,
All earth can take or heaven can give …

In apocalyptic mood, Yeats could as vividly imagine beginnings as he could ends:

> The Roman Empire stood appalled,
> It dropped the reins of peace and war,
> When that fierce Virgin and her Star
> Out of the fabulous darkness called.

That the beginning and this the end:

> Turning and turning in the widening gyre
> The falcon cannot hear the falconer;
> Things fall apart; the centre cannot hold;
> Mere anarchy is loosed upon the world.
> The blood-dimmed tide is loosed, and everywhere
> The ceremony of innocence is drowned;
> The best lack all conviction, while the worst
> Are full of passionate intensity.

Jerusalem, Athens and Rome.

Still rummaging round in our school-bags.

Why must we continue to be imitators? Why can't we be aboriginally creative? For we are Aborigines. European Aborigines. The new astronomy, the new epistemology and the new anthropology have made us so.

We have undergone a Year One Reed.

Continuously over three centuries we have undergone it. And some there are who have undergone it to the point, very nearly, of psychic foundering. Indeed Nietzsche did founder.

And in this he is portent.

Recoil hasn't worked. Neither Nietzsche's recoil nor Arnold's recoil nor Sylvia's recoil has worked.

Our only hope, as I saw it, is in going forward, is in going forward across the Kedron into our *transtorrentem* evolution.

Jesus went beyond our Classical-Christian school-bag.

Long before we found ourselves beyond it, he had gone beyond it.

What comfort will Narada get by knocking at Homer's door? What comfort will Narada get by knocking at Isaiah's door? What comfort will Narada get by knocking at Cicero's door?

The Good News is, Christ has gone on from where we find ourselves. Where we find ourselves is where Sylvia finds herself:

> My bones hold a stillness, the far
> Fields melt my heart.
> They threaten
> To let me through to a heaven
> Starless and fatherless, a dark water.

Crossing the Kedron is recovery. And if we were sapient we would ritualize that recovery and, praying in a new way, we would let a new culture emerge and cohere around it. Then again, in Yeats image, we will have a centre that will hold.

What a long detour it has been, from Bit Akitu to the *Pequod*, from *Enuma Elish* to 'Sheep in Fog'.

Having vested everything, even our very identities, in the detour, finding our way back to the evolutionary Trail won't be easy. Melville has scripted the alternative, a vortex in the dark water. (*Nostos*, pp. 597–600)

*

Our greatness, if we can call it such, is not in fabrication, in making and using tools. It is not in the domestication of fire, not in the domestication of animals, not in the invention of the wheel or in the cultivation of cereals and root crops. Greater than all of these is the fact that, after dreadful errancy, we have found our way back to the evolutionary trail, to

BRIGHT ANGEL TRAIL

Our task now is to culturally select and submit to final evolutionary transitions.

I imagine two images of Bright Angel, one by Leonardo, the other by Rublev. In both images he is shown waiting for Christ on the floor of the Karmic Canyon. It is a moment of precarious expectancy for the whole evolutionary past and the whole evolutionary future of the Earth.

The wonder of it, an angel newly come among us, an angel brighter than any we have ever so far known, and he presiding over a humanity new in doing, new in deeds and, in time quite possibly therefore, new in nature.

I think of him as tough looking. A tough-looking Glory.

Always, when they meet on his trail, it is the rattlesnake, sensing Transcendence, although not with his forked tongue, who gives way.

Having only ever painted beautiful angels, Leonardo and Rublev have their work cut out for them.

And how able for Bright Angel would Abraham have been?

How able for Bright Angel would Jacob have been?

If he was the angel who heard him and answered him, how able for Bright Angel would Rilke have been?

Gone down following Bright Angel into the Canyon, how able are any of us for the karmic cup and the self-naughting Nunatak?

More challenging than any other angel who has previously come among us, to challenge us, is Bright Angel. He challenges us back on to the evolutionary trail, this time in the expectation and hope of finality.

The question is, how many of us will let evolutionary finality come upon us, in the Canyon? How many of us are willing to go beyond that in us that evolves?

That in us that evolves isn't all that we are.

First we become all that we are, then we stand willing to lose it, all of it, all of it that is losable.

God as Divine Ungrund in us isn't losable.

Divine Ungrund, Divine Mirum.

On the Nunatak that rises above dualizing mind and self-seeking in us we pray:

May I be as out of your way awake, God, as I am in dreamless sleep.

It is as absence of self that I present myself to you, God. (*What the Curlew Said*, p. 303)

*

I delight in Him, Jesus walking the roads of Judaea shattering our world – with parables.

*

As I understand Him and know Him, Jesus emerging from His Passion is the first Buddh Gaiain.

*

It wasn't only once or twice in my adult life that I was happy to be congregationalized. I was happy to go with the traditional flow of things at my father's funeral and again more recently in Dublin. I was staying with Marie and Michael and Martin Hughes in their house beside the Four Courts. I had a bag of chemotherapy strapped to me. It would take forty-eight hours or so to infuse. That was after two other bags of it in hospital that day. It was the fourteenth of June, St Anthony of Padua's feast day, and Marie insisted that I would celebrate the occasion with them, so I crossed the Liffey with them to Adam and Eve's, a Franciscan church on Merchant's Quay. I was of course aware that the hospital

I was in that morning was located at 7 Eccles Street, an address famous in *Ulysses* and here I was now five or six words adrift in *Finnegans Wake*.

The Army Band was there to entertain a huge gathering of people, many of them having standing room only. As though they were being played by Michelangelo's apocalyptic angels, the first few trumpet blasts were tremendous and terrible. Not only was I listening to the suddenly erupting gable in the Sistine Chapel, I was for a while caught up in the descending, doomed tumult of it. In the silence between more hopeful hymns, Marie leaned across my lap and talked to Andrew, her young nephew, about the many miracles that St Anthony had performed. He was one day preaching to a congregation who showed no interest at all in what he was saying. 'Right,' he said, 'I will bother ye no further. I'll go down and teach these eternal truths to the fish in the river.' The pure foolishness of the idea aroused everyone's attention, so down they went with him and, to their utter astonishment, the fish came to his call and, crowded there in the pool at his feet, they not only listened to him, in their behaviour afterwards it was obvious that they had heard and heeded him. Another day, in conversation with him, a local lord declared that he didn't believe that Christ was really present in the consecrated Eucharistic elements. 'Here's what you'll do,' St Anthony said. 'Having starved him for a week, bring your mule to me.' This the lord did. Coming out to meet them, St Anthony had an armful of hay in one hand and a consecrated Host in a monstrance in the other. Hungry as he was, the mule went down on his knees before the Host. Leaving it at that for now, Marie pointed to a shrine within the church. 'These and other miracles are depicted on its walls,' she said, 'and we will go over and look at them after the ceremony.' This we did but, before that as she talked, leaning across my lap, I sensed that the mule in me had gone down on his knees before Christ, that the Minotaur in me had gone down on his knees before Christ, that Chiron the Centaur in me had gone down on his knees before Christ. More abstractly, I sensed that my inner phylogenetic ancient regime had gone down on its knees before Christ. This was my French Revolution, and the only difference between me and the Minotaur was that his beastliness had outcropped more obviously in him than mine had in me.

When, more than forty years ago, I was a student here in Dublin, I walked these streets, up and down Fish Shambles Street, back along the quay past this church, up along Parliament Street to Dublin Castle, west to Christ Church Cathedral and back again along the river. Since it was in Fish Shambles Street that Handel's *Messiah* was first performed I inwardly and apocalyptically heard the apocalyptic declaration:

And He shall reign for ever and ever.

He, the Messiah.
Messiah and Minotaur.
In Gethsemane the Messiah experienced and lived all of our darkest impulses. He experienced and lived them

innocently and so, when I arrive at the gates of heaven and I am morally X-rayed there, I will look at the screen and say, Yes, everything that appears there is true of me, but I have news for you God, in the person of Jesus you yourself have lived them all innocently and now, claiming that innocence, I will, if I graciously may, walk in.

The Beast in me on his knees before his own innocence in Jesus.

The Minotaur in me on his knees before his own innocence in Messiah.

> And He shall reign for ever and ever.

That an apocalyptic wonder to go down to the river and talk to the fish about, that an apocalyptic wonder to go down along Bright Angel Trail and talk to trilobite and ammonite about.

Chemotherapy and Christian therapy.

Therapy in a hospital for what, if only at face value, is a physical ailment, therapy in a church for moral and spiritual ailments. (*What the Curlew Said*, pp. 367–9)

Call it
Slí na Fírinne
Call it
The Adventure of Our Immortality
As
Jesus Pioneered It

It began in egressus:

Et egressus est Jesus cum discipulis suis trans torrentem
    Cedron.
And Jesus went forth with his disciples over a torrent
    called the Kedron.

And they came to a place which was named Gethsemane: and he saith to his disciples, sit ye here, while I shall pray. And he taketh with him Peter and James and John, and began to be sore amazed and to be very heavy.

Sore amazed by what he knows.

What the Psalmist knows he knows;

> I am fearfully and wonderfully made.

What Heraclitus knows he knows:

> You would not find the boundaries of the soul, even by travelling along every path, so deep a measure does it have.

What Jacob Boehme knows, he knows:

> In man is all whatsoever the sun shines upon or heaven contains, also hell and all the deeps.

What Sir Thomas Browne knows, he knows:

> There is all Africa and her prodigies in us.

What William Law knows, he knows:

> Thy natural senses cannot possess God or unite thee to Him; nay, the inward faculties of understanding, will and memory, can only reach after God, but cannot be the place of His habitation in thee. But there is a root or depth in thee whence all these faculties come forth as lines from a centre, or as branches from the body of the tree. This depth is called the centre, the fund or bottom of the soul. This depth is called the unity, the eternity – I had almost said the infinity – of thy soul, for it is so infinite that nothing can satisfy it or give rest but the infinity of God.
>
> This time of disputing and speculating upon ideas is short; it can last no longer than whilst the sun of this world can refresh your flesh and blood, and so keep the soul from knowing its own depth or what has been growing in it. But when this is over, then you must know and feel what it is to have a nature as deep and strong and large as eternity.

What William Wordsworth knows, he knows:

>   Not chaos, not
> The darkest pit of lowest Erebus,
> Nor aught of blinder vacancy scooped out
> By help of dreams – can breed such fear and awe
> As fall upon us often when we look
> Into our Minds, in the Mind of Man –

What Baudelaire knows, he knows:

Homme libre, toujours tu cheriras la mer;
La me rest ton miroir; tu contemples ton ame
Dans le deroulement infini de sa lame
Et ton esprit n'est pas un gouffre moins amer.

What Hopkins knows, he knows:

O the mind, mind has mountains, cliffs of fall
Frightful, sheer, no-man-fathomed ...

What Emerson knows he knows:

It is the largest part of man that is not inventoried. He has many enumerable parts: he is social, professional, political, sectarian, literary, in this or that set or corporation. But after the most exhausting census has been made, there remains as much more which no tongue can tell. And this remainder is that which interests.

What Nietzsche discovered, he knows:

I have discovered for myself that the old human and animal life, indeed the entire prehistory and past of all sentient being, works on, loves on, hates on, thinks on in me.

What Conrad knows, he knows:

The mind of man is capable of anything- because everything is in it, all the past as well as all the future.

What William James knows he knows:

> The further limits of our being plunge, it seems to me, into an altogether other dimension of existence from the sensible and the merely understandable.

What D.H. Lawrence knows he knows:

> There is that other universe, of the heart of man
> that we know nothing of, that we dare not explore.
> A strange grey distance separates
> our pale mind still from the pulsing continent
> of the heart of man.
>
> Fore-runners have barely landed on the shore
> and no man knows, no woman knows
> the mystery of the interior
> when darker still than Congo or Amazon
> flow the heart's rivers of fullness, desire and distress.

What Rilke knows he knows:

> However vast outer space may be, yet with all its sidereal distances, it hardly bears comparison with the dimension, with the depth dimension, of our inner being, which does not even need the spaciousness of the universe to be within itself almost unfathomable. (*Slí na Fírinne*, pp. 2–5)

*

A Bright Angel Trail of mahavakyas and to have set deinanthropic foot on it and to have walked down along it, that already is to have found one's way, as Jesus did, to the floor of the Canyon, that already is to be sore amazed and very heavy, already that is
Passion

It is the one, vast, simultaneous adventure of who we phylogenetically and immortally are because as Sir Thomas Browne reminds us:

> There is surely a piece of Divinity in us, something that was before the Elements and owes no homage unto the Sun. (*Slí na Fírinne*, p. 2–6)

*

Next day, as on the self-naughting Nunatak still within the Canyon, at a height where I is we, where the individual is cosmic compendium, he looked down into the universal empty skull and there it is now
Buddh Gaia
brightening the universe

Our creed is simple:
Jesus is the world's new story

All the way forward from its beginnings it is a

NEW WORLD

And the challenge to us is

INNOVATION

fully acknowledging that Jesus geologically endured the evolutionary mutation of the Labyrinth into Bright Angel Trail,

fully acknowledging that Jesus has claimed the whole Canyon for culture, the whole psyche for sanctity. (*Slí na Fírinne*, p. 21)

*

Whether Christianity recognizes it or not, Gethsemane isn't only atonement. Atonement in the sense of appeasement or expiation, I mean. As Jesus experienced it, Gethsemane is a recapitulation of evolution. (*Turtle Was Gone a Long Time, Volume One: Crossing The Kedron*, p. xxx)

*

… I heard the drip drip drip drop drop of water being poured into wine and, soon afterwards, the sound of the dry crisp bread being broken.

The most serious sounds in Christendom, I thought.

For a Christian, these, the sounds of the universe being redeemed, must surely be the next most serious sounds since the sounds of creation …

The sounds with which God called the universe into being and now in this little chapel the sound of water being poured and the sound of bread being broken, these the sounds of that same universe being redeemed.

It was terrible because, heard in another way, these were the sounds of the universe turning back, as upon an axle, towards its Divine Source. Christ was the axle, the living axle, and the turning upon Him was screeching agony.

At home in north Kerry when we were young we would sometimes hear such a screech on the road outside our house. If Maag Mahony or Dan Quin or Moss Hartnett hadn't greased the axle of their ass cart or horse cart, then the turning of the wheels upon it would issue in screech after screech after screech all the way from Poll to Moyvane.

No different, I had often supposed, was Christ's *axis mundi* screech on Golgotha.

The minister spoke the Eucharistic Prayer.

He received.

We received, saying, as the bread and wine were given to us:

Lamb of God, you who take away the sins of the world, Have mercy on us. (*Serious Sounds*, pp. 25–7)

*

Gethsemane is a meeting of the waters. It is where history, errant for so long, flows back into evolution. (*Night Journey to Buddh Gaia*, p. 424)

*

Paradise regained is in part paradisal perception regained. Or gained maybe for the first time. (*Night Journey to Buddh Gaia*, p. 432)

*

As exigently as we need our senses we need a new sensibility. We need a new way of being sensate, of being sensible to things.

Think of Thomas Traherne's childhood sensibility:

> The corn was orient and immortal wheat, which never should be reaped, nor was ever sown. I thought it had stood from everlasting to everlasting. The dust and stones of the street were as precious as gold: the gates were at first the end of the world. The green trees when

I saw them first through one of the gates, transported and ravished me, their sweetness and unusual beauty made my heart to leap, and almost mad with ecstacy, they were such strange and wonderful things. The Men! O what venerable and reverend creatures did the aged seem! Immortal Cherubims! And young men glittering and sparkling Angels, and maids strange seraphic pieces of life and beauty! Boys and girls tumbling in the street, and playing, were moving jewels. I knew not that they were born or should die; but all things abided eternally as they were in their proper places. Eternity was manifest in the Light of Day, and something infinite behind everything appeared: which talked with my expectation and moved my desire. The city seemed to stand in Eden, or to be built in Heaven …

This is silver-branch perception and, moving from the perceiver to things perceived, it is silver-branch ontology.

It is what Manannán sang of at sea and, given our continuing ecological havoc, it must surely help were we to inherit Manannán's song as a Song of God, as a Bhagavad Gita.

Silver-branch ontology and the feelings and moral awareness that go with it would of themselves constitute a new sensibility. It will of course be objected that such a sensibility is wholly unrealistic. The truth is otherwise: given the havoc it so happily permits, it is current sensibility that is unrealistic. It is good neither for us nor for the Earth that our eyes are economic brain tumours: we look at a tree and, instead of seeing it as Traherne in his early years would see it, we see timber. Looking at a cow we see kilos of meat and gallons of milk. Looking at ourselves we see industrial manhours and workforce by the trainload. (*Night Journey to Buddh Gaia*, p. 432–3)

*

As for our secular world – in our sometimes revolutionary efforts to build a Europia we have built a Utopia, a no place going nowhere. In it, our diagnoses being what they are, our remedies are what they are, guillotine and Gulag being the most immediate but not the most serious and lasting side effects.

And, under the in-fluence of Ahab's sea-grey grog, as almost all of us are, it never once occurred to Ishmael, not even when he was at the helm, to bring the *Pequod* round. (*Night Journey to Buddh Gaia*, p. 582)

Walking Beautifully on the Earth

(John Moriarty's Relationship with Nature)

On Wednesday, 2 February 1938 John Moriarty was born in the end room at home in a thatched cottage that had neither electricity nor piped water, on a small farm outside Moyvane in north Kerry. John grew up there in open countryside observing and noticing everything in nature. He developed a reflective and inquisitive mind.

He was quite content to ramble through the fields on his own marvelling at glorious coloured wild flowers coming up out of brown earth. He recalls one Christmas Eve, when he was five, listening to the sound of the lapwings in the field beside the house. For John's family God was Rí na nDúl *(king of the elements). They were interdependent with nature, falling in with its rhythms, saving hay, cutting turf, ploughing the land and milking cows.*

John knew his neighbours and their traits and characteristics living in this land of folktales and superstition. He enjoyed simple pastimes like searching for birds' nests in the hedges with his friend Tom or hunting for eels in the river.

When he moved to Canada in adult life the climate and landscape were entirely different from what he knew at home. One evening, travelling with friends on the Trans-Canada Highway towards the Rockies, he was spellbound by the Northern Lights that turned their car into a chariot of fire.

He reflected on the North American rivers. One of them, the Assinboine, flowed right behind his house and he was amazed by how unmanifest it was. In New Mexico he was delighted to be in touch with real red earth instead of Canadian snow.

He came back to Ireland to seek his bush soul outside of society. He wanted to remake his mind and spirit through conscious sensorial contact with nature as it is in itself with no distortion by intention or purpose. He was symphonic with nature and noticing its every detail with full awareness and appreciation and learning its secrets and wonders. He could then walk beautifully on the earth. He was on a vision quest trying to make sense of life and of the universe. Even when hauling in lobster pots off the coast of Inisbofin he had a singing sense of the universe.

One day he was fortunate to meet Lynne Hill and he rented a lovely cottage from her at the foot of Derrada Hill. It mirrored a pool where ocean and river meet. It sheltered him in his most difficult depths for it was a house at peace with the earth it stood on. Here he could grow in wisdom intuited by heart and senses and imagination deeper than thought. Now he was empowered to devise an alternative culture for healing the earth.

He spent long hours on the mountains or by a waterfall, getting to know it with eyes closed – just intense listening and keen hearing until there was no difference between subject and object and all selfhood gone, there was no John. Then opening his eyes getting to know the same waterfall by sight. Doing this six days in a row frightened him when he realized his very existence was unaccountable.

Out here on the mountains John coined the word thaumophany *to describe the bewondering of the world in glorious landscapes and in all living creatures. He proclaimed that matter is mind in hibernation. Now he could see and know everything in the world in a totally new way with a barefoot heart and a barefoot brain. Everything here was holy as the Burning Bush of Moses, and it was emanating from the Other world. He knew this in the 'deep heart's' core. Waking up to the ordinary and seeing the pure wonder of it was his Easter morning. He had a centre that would hold.*

Lapwings I remember. My mother lighting the lamp and in the field in front of the house lapwings calling, every call a complaint. Or so it seemed to me. And the wonder was that even when they were being battered by hailstones they didn't alter their complaints. They neither lengthened nor deepened them. In all weathers, and at all hours of the night, their complaints were as elegant as their crests.

    What saddened me is that they were so frightened of me. I only had to walk into the field and instantly they would become a flock of shimmerings swiftly swerving as they flew and then, as though quenching themselves, they would land farther off, among the rushes maybe, where I'd no longer be able to see them.

That's what had happened this evening, but now again at nightfall they had come back to the richer feeding grounds beside the house and that I was glad of because if ours was a house that lapwings could come close to, then surely also it was a house that angels would come close to.

Surely tonight they would come close because since darkness had begun to fall this was Christmas Eve and Madeleine my oldest sister was singing 'Silent Night, Holy Night', and Chris had brought two bags of turf from the shed, and Babs had brought two buckets of water from the well, and already, its flame perfectly calm, the lamp was giving more light than the fire, its raptures big and small.

But lamplight and firelight, that was every night.

Tonight was different.

Looking at the crib in the deep sill of our front window, I could see that the light of the highest heaven was in our house.

It was a night of wonders. (*Nostos*, p. 5)

*

Cutting turf every year in the bog, we worked our way down into a world no human being had ever set foot on. By midday every day for five days we would be uncovering the floor of an ancient pine forest. The preserved tree stumps and trunks we'd uncover we called bogdeal. Sometimes the bark of a trunk we'd uncover would be as distinct as it was on the day it fell, frightening birds or deer into flight. Of one thing we could be sure, and that was that it fell long before even the most mythic of our ancestors walked here. And since Ireland is a country, and since, like every other country, it came into existence with the peoples who came here and settled here, then it followed that the tree stumps we uncovered were older than it.

I didn't know it in any very conscious way then but I now know that this sacrament of going down below history had, by the time I was ten years old, given a direction, never afterwards much altered, to my life.

But we didn't only stand deeper than Ireland in the bog. We sat deeper than Ireland by our fire. (*Nostos*, p. 7)

*

A few months later, in April, Tom Welsh and myself were coming up the road. We had cuttings Dan Scanlan had given us. Reaching the brow of Fitz's Hill we recognized a woman everyone feared coming down towards us in her ass and cart. Terrified that she would put the evil eye on them, we dropped the cuttings and to make sure we were out of harm's way we climbed through the fence where there was a break in the hawthorn hedge and went off searching for bird's nests.

By the middle of May that year we had discovered forty-six nests, and these were the nests that were difficult to find, the nests of blackbirds, thrushes, wagtails, wrens, robins, larks, wild duck, snipe and, most difficult of all, the nests of goldfinches – three of them in the old apple trees of Paddy Aherne's orchard.

Every evening after school that's what we did. We went off to keep track of what was happening in these nests. On Saturdays, and again on Sundays, we would be out for most of the day.

Often, we would hear people saying that the countryside we lived in wasn't fit for man or beast. Mary Ann Danny O' was famous because, talking one day to a woman who had called to see her, she said, 'Isn't it a lonely place I am living in, and isn't it lonely I am myself looking out this door and seeing nothing coming towards me always but the blowin' wind and the wet rain?'

Maag Mahony, who lived in Poll, a place almost as desolate, agreed. 'Yes,' Maag said, 'there are days when I look through my door and the only thing I can say about the wind is that it is blowin' and the only thing I can say about the rain is that it is wet. (*Nostos*, p. 10)

*

How strange it was that we who so happily tormented Mary Ann were so tender towards nesting birds. Never once, by too sudden an approach, did we frighten a bird off her eggs. Never once, by lingering too long, did we make a hatching bird uneasy. Never once, by over-forcing our way to a nest, did we leave evidence of intrusion behind us. Rather than cause the slightest upset, we were happy to walk away not knowing what we would otherwise have liked to have known. And this paid off, because, to a quite remarkable degree, it fostered an intuitive sense of our surroundings in us. It was as if our oldest ancestors had whispered to us. In the stealth of our walking and, above all, in a kind of complicity with things, we were on the way to becoming good hunters.

Like good hunters, there was much that we knew.

At a glance we could distinguish a blackbird's nest from a thrush's nest. At a glance we could distinguish a linnet's egg from a yellowhammer's egg. And we knew where not to search for a snipe's nest or a wild duck's nest.

And because we couldn't see them perhaps, few things we did gave us such silent delight as to insert a finger into a wren's nest and feel five eggs, and then, to insert it again a few days later and feel five chicks.

For want of a good terrier, and a good greyhound, we didn't hunt foxes and hares and rabbits. (*Nostos*, p. 11)

*

It was unfortunate for eels that they looked as they did, that they felt as slimy in the hand as they did.

Our hunting ground was a reach of river from Paddy Aherne's to Danny Shaun's.

Apart from an acquired sense of where we could find them, under large, loose stones in the shallows, we didn't know much about eels.

To us they were a kind of shrivelled or degenerate water snake, and that gave us a right to be savage towards them. …

We took on the Snake that had engulfed us. We took him on where we knew we would find him, under loose stones in the shallows of our river.

We hunted him with table forks and our glee was unconfined when we hung him aloft, gasping and wriggling, in the sunlight.

We might have been poor, someone might have put bad eggs in our hay and, following up on that all but two of our cows might have slung their calves, but in spite of that we were still alive, we were willing to live, and days there were when, coming home from the river, we were heroes. In the way that Michael the Archangel was a hero, we were heroes. (*Nostos*, p. 12–13)

*

More often than not now, I'd go off through the fields on my own. There were fields that I loved. Fields with a sward of natural, wild herbs. In the Hill Meadow I saw hints of Paradise. It was the only name I had for the flowers that grew there, primroses and cowslips in the dry parts of it and in the more marshy parts, buttercups and orchids.

And I wondered.

How could something so yellow as a buttercup come up out of brown soil? How could something so purple as an orchid come up out of it? How could something so perfect as a cowslip come up out of it?

Where did the colour and the perfection come from?

And what else was down there?

What else was I walking on?

To me to inhale the fragrance of a primrose was a Eucharist.

A Eucharist without suggestion of bloodshed or blood.

Sometimes I'd inhale the fragrance down to the very soles of my feet. Then I could walk the earth without hurting it. Then I could walk in Paradise. Right here in our own Hill Meadow, I could walk in Paradise.

It was a strange world of orchids and piseogs.

It was a strange world of cowslips and bad meat.

I often thought about the priest who had preached against piseogs. On the following Saturday night, when he went into his confession box to hear and forgive the sins of his people, he sat down on thirteen rotten eggs. (*Nostos*, p. 12–13)

*

Sometimes it will happen. We carry on for years making do with a habitual sense of ourselves. Then there comes a night when we dream a tremendous dream or when we are dreamed by a tremendous dream. As if the psyche felt demeaned by being taken so much for granted, it puts on a spectacular. Waking, we acknowledge that we didn't know ourselves at all, and from now on, for weeks or for months maybe, we have a new and fearful, even a reverent respect for who we are. It was like this one night in Saskatchewan. I was in the back seat of a car travelling west with some friends along the Transcanada Highway to the Rockies. Emerging from a slightly numbed state of mind, I became aware of light in the car. It was a living, flaming light. Alarmed, I sat up. 'What's going on?' I asked. 'Are we on fire or what?' 'No, no,' the girl at the wheel said. 'It's the world that's on fire. It's the Northern Lights, look out through your window.'

Would you please stop? I asked, having caught a glimpse of them.

She pulled over. I opened the door and stepped out, no, not onto the earth but into the galaxy, into the fire and light of the galaxy, the galaxy opening and closing its curtains of fire and light, curtains of amber light moving behind curtains of fox-coloured light, all of Saskatchewan fox-coloured and my thoughts and my feelings fox-coloured, and the earth, our earth, a gorgeous astronomical scandal to stars that aren't suns, to stars that have no planets. And how sad I was for stars that aren't suns, for stars that aren't circled by seven planets, some of them sometimes passing through meteor showers, some of them showered by auroras.

No, Laplace, no, no, no, no!

Here in Saskatchewan tonight I cannot see the celestial machine you saw. Watching the curtains of fire and light moving before and behind each other, I cannot put *mecanique* and *celeste* together and then pleased with myself, sit back and think, now I've explained the heavens.

Tonight in Saskatchewan the naked eye sees what the conceptualizing eye cannot see. It sees and it knows that the heavens are dancing outside our astronomies, it sees and it knows that the cosmos is dancing outside our cosmologies.

Never till tonight did I see that the universe is much more a thing of fire than it is a thing of earth or air or water.

Essential to life they might be, but earth, air and water seemed to me now to be little more than local aberrations that didn't stand a chance.

How tremendous the universe is, I thought.

Tremendous in the little water-walking spider who comes home with a cultural alternative to Western Titanism.

Tremendous in the Arctic shaman who leaves his body and sets out on the trail to the floor of the ocean, to the floor of the psyche.

Tremendous in the girl who, having learned it from the buffalo, enacts *we-awareness* among us.'

'Tremendous in a blizzard that turns a university in which quantum mechanics and genetics are taught into a village of igloos.

Tremendous in auroras that turn a car travelling west to the Rockies into a chariot of fire.

Within an hour it was the street lights of Moose Jaw, pitiful by comparison, that illuminated us.

The street lights of Swift Current illuminated us.
The street lights of Medicine Hat illuminated us.

- Coming west across the world behind us, dawn caught up with us as we climbed through the foothills beyond Calgary. And how shocking it was that the Transcanada Highway didn't do something, didn't turn aside and submit to a purifying sweat in an Indian sweat-lodge, before it streaked so heedlessly onward into the Rockies. How shocking that it didn't turn round on itself and do a prostrate figure of eight, figure of infinity. How shocking that it didn't go north and sit for one whole moon in his initiating igloo with Igjugarjuk.

A month in that igloo might make a trail of it. A trail able to cross Saskatchewan, but not with the intention of getting anywhere. A trail able to find its own geomantic way, not our engineered way, among the mountains.

As it was, the Transcanada Highway might as well be a wake of the *Pequod*, and that was strange, because my reason for going west was to let the Kwakiutl have their say, their Tsetsekia say, in my soul, and to this end I had it in mind, over a week or so, to walk the wild Pacific coasts they once lived on.

For now, however, the Rocky Mountains rose up between me and those sea coasts and although I didn't have exact geological knowledge of them, I felt I could safely assume that in Jurassic, Ordovician or Silurian times past these summits were sea-floors and, snow covered though they were, in terrible, unthinkable shoulders of rock they here and there showed forth these ancient profundities. And how strange it was, for normally we think of looking down into profundities – here we looked up at them, here we look up and see what we have come up out of. But then of course Nietzsche discovered that it is only in a most precarious and subversible way that we have come up, for all those old sea-floors have come up with us, have come up in us, and there they were savagely shining and savagely shadowed above the lonesome timber-line. And it wasn't a lapse into a logger's hardheadedness to call it the timber-line, for it was only by turning themselves into needled timbers that trees could put their own *rigor mortis* to such flourishing good use here.

How like a Greek theatre, that corrie. And yet it was unthinkable that we would stage either our salvation or damnation up there. Up there on those shining white summits, on summits serene beyond condescension or disdain, it would be simply fantastical to imagine that our welfare or woe counted for anything.

That's how Wallace Stevens imagined us. He imagined us as the transparence of the place in which we are. (*Nostos*, p. 261–2)

*

Back in Winnipeg in September, I moved to the upper floors of an old house on Assiniboine Avenue.

There is something more than poetry in the native names of North American rivers – the Missouri, the Mississippi, the Cheyenne, the Shenandoah, the Susquehanna and, behind my rooms now, a yard and a small wilderness away, the Assiniboine.

The Assiniboine has its source in central Saskatchewan. Joined by a tributary that has its source near Moose Jaw, it flows all the way east till it meets the Red and then turns north into Lake Winnipeg.

Flowing through land traditionally occupied by the Assiniboine People, it is a silent river. It was hard to imagine how it could exist and yet draw so little attention to itself. For me that was its mystery.

Along its course, from source to sea, the Colorado River drops by as many as ten thousand feet. That means that along some of its reaches it is a loud river, a roaring river.

A river of the Northern Plains, the Assiniboine doesn't roar. Entering the lake, it doesn't beat a drum and sing its own death-song.

It intrigued me.

To be or not to be, that according to Hamlet is the question, only of course it isn't the question. Certainly for an Assiniboine warrior it isn't the question.

I would imagine him.

Dressed in beaded moccasins, in liturgically spectacular buckskins, in a headdress of eagle feathers, holding a ritually empowered spear and a ritually empowered shield— for him mere existence is not the question. For him the question is, how magnificent in the way that mountains and rattlesnakes are magnificent can I be, how terrifyingly visible can I be, how out of proportion to what I might actually be can I be?

Sitting Bull is my name.

Red Cloud is my name.

Rolling Thunder is my name.

Is that what life is? I would sometimes wonder. Is it a will to be magnificently manifest? Manifest now and manifest after death? And that will, that will to be magnificently manifest, does it animate the daisy, the day's eye, as much as it does the Plains warrior?

It might be so.

Only it isn't so for the Assiniboine River.

Flowing through our town, the Assiniboine doesn't only represent the Unmanifest to us, it is the Unmanifest among us.

It is *moksha*, it is liberation, from the Manifest.

It is *moksha* from the will to be manifest.

Only one more thing you must do, Alice. Having looked up into the tree and seen only the grin, you must now stand on Assiniboine Bridge and look east along the river. Being the Unmanifest, or being as un manifest as anything that still exists can possibly be, it is our sutra, it is our upanishad. What the *Kena Upanishad* apophatically says, it says. Speaking of or for the Unmanifest it says:

> There goes neither the eye, nor speech, nor the mind, we know it not, nor do we know how to teach one about it. Different it is from all that is known and beyond the unknown it also is.

Wonderful that such a river flows all the way east across the Northern Plains.

Wonderful that such a river still flows east, orientally east, behind my house.

Wonderful that the frightful advertising visibilities of Pembina Highway, visibilities that seek to persuade us to put a tiger in our tank or to smoke Rothman's cigarettes – wonderful that here in loud Winnipeg there is such a silent river.

Wonderful that here in Winnipeg the will to be manifest doesn't have things all its own way.

The first night I spent in my new rooms, that's what I thought about. I thought about the choice Siddhartha made between Pembina Highway and the Assiniboine River.

That choice transformed Asia. And it is also possible that it will also transform the West.

Twice already since I came to Winnipeg it had happened. Precipitated neither by nightmare nor by dream, I had woken up to infinite nothingness. On both occasions the experience was momentary. Strange to say, the nothingness didn't seem like *nihil*.

What you say about Old Man River is right, Paul.

> He must know somethin
> He don't say nothin

Although flowing through the world he must mirror the world, what he most deeply knows he knows at source, and he knows it re-entering the sea.

The Yukon, the Saskatchewan, the Assiniboine, the Mississippi, the Missouri, the Cheyenne, the Susquehanna, the Shenandoah.

It was the first song I sang in my new living-room:

> O Shenandoah, I long to see you,
> Away, you rolling river.
> O Shenandoah, I long to see you,
> Away I'm bound to go
> Across the wide Missouri …

America! (*Nostos*, p. 271–2)

*

Days there are, though, in Manitoba, winter days there are, when all of reality is unsheathed, and you, too, you stand there drawn out of all the nonsense that has accumulated anatomically in you, you stand there drawn out of all the nonsense and ignorance that has accumulated sensually and cerebrally in you, and until today you thought that Excalibur was a sword but now you know that, drawn out of its worldly eclipse of itself, *every sun beam is a sonnebeame more clearer by seven tymys than ever they saw day.* In Manitoba, today there is no eclipse, and when you meet them you tell your friends who are physicists that the vibrations they study are hosannas, for that is what Excalibur is, it is the eternally praising brightness you'd walk in walking to work on a winter's morning in Winnipeg.

>All of this
>>in the land of the Manitou
>All of this
>>Although no one cried for a vision

What a great day it was, the day Sir Gawayne came to his feet in Camelot:

> 'Now,' seyde Sir Gawayne. 'We have bene servd thys day of what metys and drynkes we thought on. But one thing begyled us, that we might nat se the Holy Grayle: hit was so preciously coverd. Wherefore I woll make here a vow that to-morne, withoute longer abydygne, I shall laboure in the queste of the Sankgreall, and that I shall holde me oute a twelve-month and a day or more if need be, and never shall I returne unto the courte agayne tylle I have sene hit more opynly than hit hath bene shewed here. And if I may nat spede I shall returne agayne as he that may nat be ayenst the wylle of God.'

Vision quest in the Old World.
Crying for a vision in the New World.
Hanble ceyapi, the Sioux call it.
In the Old World or in the New World, in Arthurian times or in modern times, it is always in the single individual that humanity comes to its feet.
Thinking of all this in a motel a mountainous mile high in the Rockies, it occurred to me, remembering those Manitoba mornings, that the Diamond Sutra, that the Excalibur Sutra we have need of, we haven't yet written.

It was through high country we travelled all the way south into New Mexico. High country, and what they called Big Country. I had of course seen it in Westerns, Comanches dressed in little but war-paint communicating by smoke signals across its immense distances.

Do what Jacob did, do it here, take a red stone of this red, rocky place and set it for your pillow, and then, the sun being set, lie down and sleep, and your dream, relived and retold over thousands of years by a thousand campfires, might well in the end be the opening chapter of a new holy book.

A book that will tell us that God doesn't need to come down upon a mountain, for the mountain itself is the revelation. We only have to look at it and we will know how we should live.

South of Albuquerque, the mountain behind us, we suddenly realized that the vibrant, red world we were driving through wasn't a mirage. We actually had come below the snowline. Lloyd pulled over, and for half an hour or more we tumbled and rolled and we wrestled, rolling in twos and threes on the hard grit between the savagely jagged rocks. We were like sailors who had just set foot on land after a three-year voyage in a whale ship. We were like horses, rolling to shake off the lingering impressions of saddle and bridle, only in our case it was the confinements and restrictions of a Canadian winter that we were shaking off. In the way that a horse, having rolled, shivers the dust off its withers and flanks, we were shivering the whiteness of snow out of our minds and eyes and into them we were breathing, as though our minds were lungs and our eyes were lungs and our lives were lungs, into them we were breathing the earth browns and the earth reds, all of them vivid, all of them vibrating, in arid New Mexico.

For this alone the journey south was worth it. We were in touch with *adamah*, with red earth, in ourselves again. In search of old even ancient ground in me, I had slept on it in Greece, and now again my eyes were alive with remembered sensations of it, of *adamah*, in the orange orchards of the Peloponese, of *adamah* in the wine and oil jars in the cellars of the palace of King Minos in Knossos, of *adamah* in the church roofs of Mistra, the dark of needle-thin cypresses rising between them.

I must, I thought, I must stay in touch with adamah in me, else I'll become what I am already becoming, an intellectual. (*Nostos*, p. 372–3)

*

As we approached it in the dark the island didn't loom. Instead it looked squat and dark and withdrawn into itself. Silhouetted against the constellations, it felt like a piece of tundra that had floated south and run aground here. And the faint, low lights of the first five or six houses we saw as he came round a headland – unnamed by Babylonians, Egyptians or Greeks, they too were a constellation, only I couldn't for the moment say whether it was coming over or going below the horizon.

Rising or setting, it put me in mind of Australian astronomy. To Aborigines, stars are the campfires of the Ancestors. Stars that are near are the campfires of those who have died recently. Stars that are far away are the campfires of those who have died a long time ago.

I imagined it: All his former horror gone from him, Kepler sitting at her campfire with Cassiopeia. And Pascal, all his former terror gone from him, sitting at his campfire with Sagittarius.

It is likely, as Sir James Jeans suggested, that the river of thought does now and then run back on itself, but whether it would ever run this far back, that didn't seem credible. Even as we homed more deeply into the shelter of this little harbour here in Inisbofin, it didn't seem credible. No. The time was past when, home from the hunt, Orion would sit down and play his dijiridu to a victim of the new astronomy.

But then, as I so often did when confronted by modern reductionism, I remembered Haldane and William James, Haldane saying that the universe is queerer than we can imagine and James telling us that there should be no premature closing our account with reality.

So maybe the those early Christian monks were right? Maybe there are dimensions of our own minds and of the world that we can only enter when we have shipped our oars, when we have shipped self-will, when we have shipped all consciously conceived, all consciously pursued purposes?

It was on the tip of my tongue to say that we have access to these charmed dimensions of mind and of world only when we have shipped everything in us that makes us different from plankton, but I held back, thinking that this might be going too far.

In Galway today I had a long wait for the bus that would bring me out here to the Atlantic coast, so I took to the streets, letting them take me where they would. Coming to a bridge over the Corrib River, I looked over the parapet. There was the big rushing river itself and running parallel to it there was what I took to be an engineered, stone-embanked side-channel of it. Growing in this side-channel were drifts of weeds, each of them flowing in perfect adaptation to the flowing, lucid water. In their shapes they were beautiful, in their textures they were beautiful, in their night-green colours they were beautiful. But they were beautiful above all because they made sense.

> The great sea has set me in motion,
> Set me adrift,
> Moving me as a weed moves in the river.
> The arch of sky and mightiness of storms
> Have moved the spirit within me,
> Till I am carried away,
> Trembling with joy.

Maybe Uvavnuk's song will sing us out of dead-end rigidities. Maybe it will sing us into more hopeful evolutionary shape.

What a pity Darwin hadn't been reading the *Tao Te Ching* before he went ashore on Galapagos. What a pity the *Tao Te Ching* wasn't Darwin's prayer-book during all the time that he was writing *The Origin of Species* and *The Descent of Man*.

Early Christian monks

and

Eskimo medicine woman

Shipped oars

and

Fluent weeds in a river.

Maybe we are still in with an evolutionary chance.

And maybe that's what the Beautiful is. The Beautiful is that which is most fluently adapted to how things are.

Judged by such a standard, of course, Western humanity is hideous. Hideous because evolution has come to so rigid an end in us. (*Nostos*, p. 401–2)

*

Hauling and sowing lobster-pots off the west coast of Ireland today, the music of the Silver Branch was beginning to sound like the music of the *St Matthew Passion*.

Having fished closer to shore for some rock bream in the meantime, they started back, hauling and cleaning and re-sowing all three lines of pots. That done, we turned for home. And, as if to make sure that our ideas didn't harden into dogmas – this evening now in the west of Ireland, even to think that we were exiled from Paradise would have been a sin against how the world looked. And there was something more. Appearances this evening weren't deceptive.

I was somehow sure of it. As the world looked, so it essentially and metaphysically was.

More even than the night in Saskatchewan when the Ford car I was travelling in blazed with auroral fire, I this evening had a tremendous singing sense of the universe. As if its ultimate particles weren't particles at all, as if they were crimson hosannas, it sang in every rock, in lobster and lobster pot it sang, and I remembered and I accepted the invitation to sing with angels and archangels that comes to us out of all too resonantly red heart of the Mass:

> *et ideo cum Angelis et Archangelis, cum Thronis*
> *et Domnationibus, cumque omni militia caelistis*
> *exercitus, hymnum gloriae tuae canimus, sine fine*
> *dicentes*
>
> *Sanctus Sanctus Sanctus*
>
> *Dominus Deus Sabaoth, pleni sunt caeli et*
> *terra gloria tua,*
>
> *hosanna in excelsis*

In a sense it is what Manannán is saying: talk no more of atoms, talk of hosannas, talk no more in mathematics, talk in quavers and semi-quavers.

This evening our *Principia Mathematica* was a book of only one sentence:

> If it is to be true, talk about the universe must be talk out over the heads of Mannannán horses.

To test it I translated it downwards into everyday realities:

> Even if he is talking to you about the continuing bad weather, or worse, about the cancer that is killing him, it is out over the heads of Manannán's horses that your neighbour is talking.

No. In the universe this evening even that didn't seem outrageous. (*Nostos*, pp. 429–30)

*

Hills and high ground secluding me, I was walking up along the Owenglin River. This early in the morning the grass was still stiff with frost and every time I set down a foot I could hear the breaking of a crystalline world. And as it flowed past me, or as it tumbled and poured and collapsed down towards me, the river was something more than a gathering of water from the sides of five mountains, all of it bank-directed, rock-directed down into the sea. To look at, it was a delight of water, as if in every molecule of it that one atom of oxygen and those two atoms of hydrogen were still amazed by the strange, miraculous new thing they turned into when they came together.

Their wide-eyed amazement I could see in the wide-eyed amazement of the water.

On its own, oxygen never mirrored anything. On its own, hydrogen never mirrored anything. Oxygen and hydrogen came together, and now Muchnaght is mirrored, Ben Corr is mirrored, Ben Bán is mirrored, Ben Bruidhín is mirrored, Ben Gleniskey is mirrored. And for all I know, maybe they need to be mirrored. And maybe that's what the universe is, a need to be mirrored. And the pools in this river, maybe they are an answer to that need. And our eyes and our minds, maybe they are an answer to it also.

Could it be that we are here for a reason?

And could it be that this is why God created the universe?

Alone, and then lonely, in his eternity, he needed something to see himself in. And he being immense, only immensity could mirror him.

And maybe there is healing here in mirroring Connemara for your horror, Johannes.

And maybe there is healing here in mirroring Connemara for your terror, Blaise.

Here in mirroring Connemara maybe there is healing for everyone who has been disabled by the terrors of the new astronomy, the new anthropology and the new epistemology.

Thinking that I might follow to Owenglin all the way up into the mountains, I came to a waterfall, as much a cascade as a waterfall, and I stopped short. In the river bed, just down from the plunge-pool, there was an outcrop of rock, the water rushing either side of it. I figured out how, by jumping from one to another steeping-stone, I might get to it dryshod. Finding a surface of it that was both dry and not so jagged I sat down, well knowing that I'd be here for at least a few hours.

Closing my eyes, I found myself wanting to get to know this cascade, this fall, purely through hearing. Distinguishing them from the overall roar, and getting to know them individually, I attended in turn to each little rush and run. Even within the big collapse and fall of it I found variety. As if this was nature's *Eroica* symphony, I got to know all the instruments and what they were doing. All of the variations and all the contrapuntal comings and goings I got to know. The waterfall in all its voices, near and far, loud and not so loud, I got to know. In the end, all awareness of the difference between subject and object in abeyance, it was to hearing itself I was listening. And what an unnaturally strange experience it was, hearing. Time was when there was no hearing in the world, but then, some redundant jawbones were redesigned and put to new use, and it happened, hearing.

Hearing in the Palaeozoic.

Hearing in the Mesozoic.

Hearing in the Kainozoic.

Hearing here to day in Connemara.

Hearing here to day under a waterfall in the Owenglin River.

I listened to the strangeness.

In the end there was no me. The strangeness was listening to itself, quite without my being aware of it, there had been a transition from *I am listening* to *listening is*, from *I am hearing* to *hearing is*.

Of its own accord, no active work required, it continued a long while.

Then, a sense of selfhood returning and re-occupying the centre, I opened my eyes and now, starting all over again, I set out to get to know what was in front of me through the sense of sight.

Numerous to hearing, it was equally numerous to sight.

But how utterly different from each other were experiences of hearing and seeing.

That long, lovely pouring there in the cascade – I well remembered what it sounded like to hearing, but now, experienced in seeing, what an altogether different reality it was.

Returning to hearing and then coming back to seeing many times over, I gave myself all the time I needed to live the difference.

This sense that there is one world, I thought, is pure illusion. There are in fact as many worlds as there are ways of perceiving.

I settled into experience of seeing.

Again, but only after a long, long time, the sense of selfhood slipped away, and once more there was a transition from *I am seeing* to *seeing is*.

Time was when there was no seeing in the world. Then some cells became particularly light sensitive. Images appeared and there was something marvellously new in the world, there was seeing.

Seeing in the Palaeozoic.

Seeing in the Mesozoic.

Seeing in the Kainozoic.

Seeing here to day in Connemara.

Seeing below a waterfall in Owenglin River.

And how strange it was.
How very, very strange it was.

A day of getting to know hearing, a day of getting to know seeing.

A day of letting hearing be in the universe, a day of letting seeing be in the universe.

Six days after each other I came back.

On what turned out to be the last day for now that I would do this, I opened my eyes and like someone who had been born blind but had suddenly and without warning been given the sense of sight, like someone who had been born deaf but had suddenly and without warning been given the sense of hearing, I was frightened not just by the unaccountable strangeness of hearing and seeing, my very existence, that too unaccountable – unaccountable in that I existed and in how I existed – it frightened me.

Knowing that I had been shaken in a place deeper than my everyday sense of myself, I got up and turned for home.

The swan's nest, the hare's form and the baptismal pool in the trout stream.

No. Even at the cost of never acquiring my bush soul, I wouldn't now be going back for those final immersions.
(*Nostos*, p. 451–4)

*

Emerging from the Ballynahinch Woods, the road followed the course, it followed the turn and rush of a lovely river. At a couple of places, stretching from bank to bank there were man-made impediments of rocks and stones. Clearly, they were designed to back up the flow of water behind them so that salmon and sea trout could find their way upstream in dry weather. Standing there and watching the bog-black water flowing so suavely over the first of these impediments, I found myself wanting to whistle – in the way that the man on the hill was whistling for his dog, I wanted to whistle for Plato, I wanted him here at my side so that I could say to him, Can't you see, seeing that water, that sensuousness and soul are one wonder going down together, as one wonder, to a blessed eternity? Can't you see that the sensuous soul sight of it and the sensuous soul sound of it should be our first and our last philosophical principle?

And if Andrew Marvell was here, and if William Butler Yeats was here – of themselves they would see that, here within reach of blissful re-absorption in the sea, their dialogues of body and soul, of self and soul, had become a single, sensuous soliloquy for the authors of the Bible to hear, for the authors of the Hermetica to hear, for the authors of the Kaballa to hear.

> For sheep and stars to hear

In the end it was simple. Cycling along beside it, I felt that this river would be sensuous soul to someone who came here having no soul at all, and for that reason I decided that I'd rent the nearest available cottage to it.

Around the next turn I found myself looking, beyond the trunks of two big elms, at the black, gable-end door of that cottage.

A cottage among trees.

A cottage by an estuary.

A cottage across a narrow road from a great pool in which river and ocean meet, in which sweet water from among the mountains and salt water from beyond the headlands become a single surprise mirroring a little island overhung on its near side by a spreading oak.

Yes, I said to Lynne, who owned it, I'd be happy to take it, but given that the Buddha's *udana* was still so present to my mind it was not without a sense of something almost foreordained that I noticed an incipient dilapidation in its windows and doors, also in the creak and sag of some of its floor-timbers downstairs and in its dormer rooms upstairs. It had, as well, a damp feel about it. On its walls it had old collectors' items, old pictures and old prints. On them also were some antelope horns, and three fox heads, all three of them snarling, the one in the living-room almost audibly. Certainly, the cottage had character. More than anything else though it had a great open fireplace, and if only for that reason I couldn't have wished for anything better.

A tractor-trailer of turf that I bought from Steven Mullins gone on ahead of me, I cycle over and moved in on the shortest day of the year.

A stables that had been converted to three physically continuous cottages, mine was at the near end and through its gable-end door it shared a walled-in yard with the big house. Steven had tipped up the turf at the mouth of a shed in this yard and my first job was to take it in and to stack it against a side wall. Lynne and Veronica, a friend of hers, came out to help me. Afterwards they invited me in for tea.

Cycling past this house my first impression of it was that it had taken on the shape and the mood of someone's Halloween dream of it. But this wasn't only true of the house. Under Derrada Hill and beside the estuary, the whole place, including the trees and the outhouses and the cottage, had a Halloween feel to it. Sitting in the warmth of its kitchen now, however, I had an altogether different sense of it. Solid and strong, there was in it a sense of friendship with the earth, of earth and house being a peace with each other. Houses now being built can only shelter us physically. Taking you as it found you, this house would shelter all of you. It would shelter you consciously and unconsciously. Dreams you might not want to dream in a new house you could dream here. Having the understanding that it has with the earth, having the permission that it has from the earth, this old house, big in its walls and big in its fires, would see you through.

Originally a private residence built by the Martins of Ballynahinch castle for one of their outside managers, Lynne was now running it as a guest house, but of course at this time of the year she had the whole place to herself, and I could see why she, a woman in her early twenties, would in these winter nights be glad to see a quiet window light shining out into the trees at the end of her long, dark yard.

Something old about this, I thought, as I walked towards my door with a bag of turf on my back. Old and serving a simple need, the need for fire and light.

In less than half an hour, I had three flames, then four, then again three, then five, all of them a lovely yellow, leaping up through the billowing smoke.

The switch on the wall beside me, I turned off the electric light. Taking its aliveness from the flames, night came back into the room. Almost palpably, my unconscious came back into my mind.

Gangasagara, Hindus call it, the place where the Ganges and the ocean meet. And here I was now sitting in a house whose firelit window was mirrored in a pool where the Owenmore and the ocean meet.

There was a verse of the *Mundaka Upanishad* that I knew. I knew it in Sanskrit:

Yatha nadyah syandamanah samudre
astam qacchanti namarupe vihaya
tatha vidvan namarupa vimuktah
paratporam purusam upaiti divyam

As rivers leaving name and form behind them
flow into their home in the ocean
so does the Knower, from name and form released,
go to that Divine Person who is beyond the beyond.

This, I could see, is something more than a drop of seal oil falling down onto our table as we stand at it kneading dough. It is something more than an invitation to dig our true identity out of the thatch, to cross the road, to drape it over our shoulders and swim away.

In metamorphosis insects undergo a transition from one to another form, from larva form to *imago* form, from being a caterpillar eating cabbage leaves to being a butterfly living on nectar.

But this is not what the *Mundaka Upanishad* is talking about. Very clearly, it is talking, not about a transition from one to another form, but about the loss of all form, of *imago* form as well as larva form. And this surely is a challenge to Christians, certainly to those Christians who look forward to a resurrection, to the acquisition in other words of an *imago* form, a bliss form, what Buddhists call the *sambhogakaya*.

I imagined it.

The Owenmore broken in stony fords and mending again into mirroring pools, pools mirroring a heron flying languidly upstream, pools mirroring a man herding sheep on Derrada Hill, pools mirroring the mists and the stars of a December night, pools expanding in rings where a salmon has leaped or an otter has dived – the Owenmore with all its rushing over rocks and between rocks, rushing over salmon eggs hatching in its coarse gravels, rushing in breaking waves around rocky, river islands and then again all mirroring ease, mirroring Lynne and Veronica out for a walk, Lynne in a blue coat, Veronica's beige, and they talking maybe about the fella who had moved into the first cottage – that the Owenmore would lose all of this, and itself as well, that, as I understood it, is what the upanishad is saying. (*Nostos*, pp. 458–60)

*

What a wonder of instinctive life it was. Flying in victories over my house, the wild geese had gone back to the tundras of Canada. And that noisy squabble of terns perched on that rock in the estuary – sure of their route in what looks like a trackless world, they have come all the way from Patagonia. The little sedge warbler has come from Africa. Swallows have come from Africa. Elvers have come from the Sargasso Sea. Salmon have come from the seas off Greenland. And finding their way by the stars, the stormy petrels have come in off the open ocean and are hatching their eggs in their old ancestral burrows.

I would think of them, the tremendous, pre-human geographies of instinct. And what a sadness of substance in us it is that we refuse to accord the dignity of intelligence to instinct, whereas instinct is life so intelligently sure of what it wants that it doesn't have to bother its head about alternatives, about a vertigo of alternatives.

And there is genius in the universe, genius that doesn't need to have recourse to the workings of the deductive intelligence. And if only we would give the genius of the universe a chance! If only we would give it a chance! Retiring to one or another of the four holy mountains is what the *wu-wei* sages of China do, and when, years later, one of them comes back down to his village, as he walks past it the dead tree blooms. As there is freezing-point in the universe so is there a miracling-point, and this old sage has found his way to it.

It's an interesting story, Columbus and Cabot, and after them Magellan, attempting to catch up with the pre-human geographies of instinct.

Ishmael gives us a sense of them:

> Alone, in such remotest waters, that though you sailed a thousand miles, and passed a thousand shores, you would not come to any chiselled hearthstone, or aught hospitable beneath that part of the sun; in such latitudes and longitudes, pursuing too such a calling as he does, the whaleman is wrapped by influences all tending to make his fancy pregnant with many a mighty birth.

Unmolested and unsubverted by fancy, the tern makes it all the way from the Falklands to Shetland. In the literal sense that it is of the order of fable, this is fabulous, and the first time I really thought about it I found myself wishing in the interests of my own safety, that I wouldn't over-awaken to the world.

Let me abide, Lord, by the chiselled hearthstone. (*Nostos*, p. 507)

*

Half way up the mountain, in an attempt to give new sight to my eyes, I coined a new word. The Greek word *thauma*, a noun, means wonder. The Greek word *phaino*, a verb, means to show, to make manifest. Putting them together, I got *thaumophany*. And that to day is what the world looked like, like wonder coming continuously out into the open, coming out as mountains, coming out as woods, coming out as rivers and herons flying home, coming out as bogs and rocks and otters, as lakes, as otter paths between lakes, coming out as stars, coming out as hearing and seeing, as the taste of a blackberry and the smell of heather.

Coming out in the way that our minds are always coming out, out into the sensations and thoughts, into sadness and hope and fear and forgiveness. In dreams in the night coming out. And what is happening in our minds is happening in rocks. It is happening in mountains.

I had somewhere read that in the Chinese language, all nouns are verbal nouns. This, if it is true, is wonderful. A speaker of English, when I see a rock I see a thing. Kuo Hsi, a speaker of Chinese, sees it as an event, or better, as an eventing, as a happening, as an action, and that might be one reason why he, also, painted mountains as though they were clouds.

Western physics has gone east to China. A wonderful thing it would be if Kuo Hsi's painting called *Early Spring* were to come west into Europe. It would recreate our eyes and minds. It would liberate rocks, mountains and rocks, from our Medousa perceptions of them. And it would un-petra-fy our languages, turning all their nouns into verbal nouns, so that our daily speech and therefore our daily awareness might at last catch up with Heraclitus and Einstein.

Today, lifting my eyes and my mind above Europe, I once again had the courage to know, and to come to know, what I knew. Looking at Ben Gleniskey across the valley from me I knew that matter isn't matter at all, it is mind in hibernation. And it might happen that I'd be cycling up along the river some morning and I'd look at the Bens but only to find that they had emerged from their hibernation and moved on.

And if Einstein was here to day he'd know that space-time is curved. Of course it is curved. Like one of those charming Cambodian Buddhas released from seemingly amorphous rock, it is sitting in the lotus position.

Again I thought of the old Zen Master. Shuffling off to bed he'd say, 'Now I'll let the trees do my thinking for me.'

That's what I was doing day to day. Climbing Ben Lettery though I was, I was letting Connemara practice *zazen* in me, not my *zazen*, its *zazen*.

Alternatively, I could do something tediously European. I could stand here and exclaim, isn't it beautiful? Aren't the woods beautiful? That way I'd be keeping Connemara at arms length. That way my immune system, psychological and epistemological, would be working only all too well. Better to climb up out of Europe. Better to let Connemara do its thinking in you, and what matter if it thinks unEuropean thoughts. Of course they will be unEuropean thoughts. But never mind. The worst that can happen is inner exile from your community.

It was Perseus who brought the Medousa mentality into Europe and for far too long too many of us have been her plenipotentiaries, reducing outwardness to *res extensa* and inwardness to *res inextensa*.

An ugly word, *thaumophany*. It was a raft that had helped me to cross a river, and I didn't now intend to sling it over my shoulders and walk overland with it. It had served a turn, but I did have one last fantasy, not about it, but about what it implied. On the sixth of January, five days from now, maybe our gift to God in epiphany should be our willingness to know and celebrate the world as a wondering and a bewondering.

I wasn't getting in touch with the mountain the way that I hoped I would. How could I? I was too busy climbing up out of Europe, the Europe whose approved ways of seeing and knowing would, in any case, have come between me and it.

To look at a tree and see timber. To look at a mountain and see matter. To look at the universe, to look at it with biblical eyes, and see handiwork.

I couldn't help it. I was climbing, but I was ghost dancing. I was ghost dancing a way of seeing out of my eyes, I was ghost dancing a way of knowing out of my mind. And as if it was written on a rock-face in front of me, I knew and could speak the divinely interrogating text:

Now Moses kept the flock of Jethro his father-in-law, the priest of Midian: and he led the flock to the backside of the desert, and came to the mountain of God, even to Hareb. And the angel of the Lord appeared unto him in a flame of fire out of the midst of a bush: and he looked and, behold, the bush burned with fire, and the bush was not consumed. And Moses said, I will now turn aside, and see this great sight, why the bush is not burnt. And when the Lord saw that he turned aside to see, God called unto him out of the midst of the bush, and said, Moses, Moses.

And Moses said, Here am I. And God said, Draw not nigh hither, put off thy shoes from off thy feet, for the place whereon thou standest is holy ground.

That's what I had attempted to do out in the bog. I had attempted, yes, to put off my shoes not just from off my feet, but from off my mind and heart. Also, I had attempted to put off their habitual, conditioned ways of seeing from off my eyes, I had attempted to put off its habitual, conditioned way of knowing from off my mind, I had attempted to walk the earth with a barefoot heart and a barefoot brain I had attempted to walk it with barefoot affections and a barefoot mind, and this I had attempted to do because, out here in Connemara how could I not have seen that all ground is holy ground, how could I not have seen that every bush is a burning bush, and how could I not have seen that stone is a-stone-ishment, introspective astonishment that keeps it from looking out and taking notice of us as a fox would or as an otter would?

I did come up on to the summit.

In a spirit of ascetic exclusion, but as sensuously as I could, I looked at one thing. I looked at a lake-brightened bog, at a bog brightened by thirty, maybe forty mirroring lakes.

I looked at it for electrons.

I looked at it for Mars.

I looked at it for the galaxy, for who can say that picking an earthworm off the road and taking him to safety mightn't make the hundred million stars of our galaxy visible to extra-galactic beings who couldn't otherwise see it.

In climbing Ben Lettery, I was attempting to climb up out of my own medulla.

What is it about houses? I wondered, sitting by the fire one night.

The house I now lived in was originally a stable, and maybe that had something to do with the fact that, asleep and awake in it, I could inhabit more of who and what I was then I could have done in any other house that I previously lived in.

Its understanding with the earth had something to do with it. On three sides of it there was rising, rocky ground, rocky, rockwalled Derrada Hill itself rising to over four hundred feet. And there were trees, not dense enough to be a wood but yet in sufficient numbers to give the impression that it was well sheltered, even closed in. Their roots having to travel a long way between and in some cases over green, moss-covered bedrock in search of soil and nourishment, some of these trees had earned the right to look as wise as they did. And then, in front, on the far side of the road, the tide coming and going. At the full, on a spring tide, the pool would expand into a lake and if there were gales or even strong winds from the south it would come out onto the road above Lynne's, leaving ebb-marks of broken reeds behind it as it retreated. Almost every day a heron would come to fish from those parts of the bank that were reed-free. In the night, now and then, I'd hear otters calling. Under hazels and an oak above in Josey Flaherty's field there was a badger set. How many badgers young and old lived in it, I didn't know. The amount of bedding they'd leave behind waiting for collection on a later night suggested quite a few. They foraged for worms in all the little fields round about, but most of all in Lynne's orchard. Every time I'd come upon one of their nose-holes in the soil, I could almost hear their little grunts of excitement and satisfaction as they located and slurped the delicious pink prey. In spite of long familiarity with them, I couldn't yet distinguish the grunt of a boar badger from that of a sow. For all I knew, they might be indistinguishable.

As well as all that I would sometimes open my gable-end door and there would be five or six horses, one of them a beautiful Palomino, in the yard. There was a sheepdog, always fussily anxious to be friendly. Her name was Ceeva. And there were two cats. One was big and soft and black and very furry. Quite out of keeping with his passive, indolent nature, and quite out of keeping also with the fact that he at all times wanted to be petted, his name was Stomper. Leaner and meaner and as red as withered savannah grass, the other was called Tiger. Both of them soon learned that I was a soft touch. They also learned that I stayed up late into the night and that I always kept a good fire on, and so, when Lynne put them out in the night, instead of going to bed in the hay, they'd come straight across the yard and call at my door.

Yet this place was by no means just the sum of its parts. It was something strangely more. But what it was I couldn't quite say. It was as if a long, long time ago it acquired the slightly mouldering appearance that it had in someone's dream of it. And it had never shaken it off. The trees hadn't. The shed's hadn't. The house outside and in some of its rooms hadn't. The orchard hadn't. Nor had the cottages.

Somehow, though, even that wasn't the whole story. From the first day I walked in by the small gate I knew that it was richer and more real than I could apprehend with my five senses. And I pictured that. Were I to dip a thermometer in water and hold it there for a while it would tell its temperature, but it wouldn't tell me whether the water was sea water or river water, whether it was flowing or at rest, whether it was clear or clouded, whether it mirrored anything, a mountain or a house. And so it was with me. In relation to the world around me and in relation to this place, my senses were wholly insufficient. Particularly was this the case on a day when I'd open my gable-end door, and the horses would turn to look at me.

And yet the place sheltered me. In a way that the Parthenon couldn't and that Chartres somehow didn't, it sheltered me in my more difficult depths. So maybe it was all very simple. It was a place under a hill and beside a river. Not just any hill, and not just any river. With all its richness of heather and furze and rockwall and rock and woodcock and turf-banks and turf and ponies and sheep, the hill was Derrada Hill and with its herons and its otters and its mirrorings and with its salmon-heaped gravels covering hatching salmon eggs and with its long, suave flowings, and with its rushing, broken flowings, no, this wasn't just any river, this was the Owenmore. I only had to walk up along it and I knew why the ancient Irish knew that all of Ireland's rivers have their source in an Otherworld Well. Depending on which story you are listening to and where it is told, this well is called Connla's Well, Nektan's Well or the Well of Segais. A hazel grows over that well, nuts drop down into it, salmon who come up into the well will sometimes carry one of those nuts downstream out of the Otherwold into our world, and anyone who finds it and drinks the *imbas* that is in it will become wise, will become a seer.

And there was an evening in the Dingle Peninsula when a stranger stopped to talk to a local man on the road outside Dunquin: It was a breathlessly silent evening. The ocean was silent. The mountains were silent. The fields were silent. The sheep and the cattle were silent. And people were silent. The only sound was the sound of a stream coming down the near side of Eagle Mountain. The stranger remarked on it. The local man listened a long while to the sound, then said, *tá sé ag glaoch orainn isteach sa tsíoraíocht as a bfhuil sé féin ag teacht*, it is calling us into the eternity and out of which it is itself flowing.

The question is, though, how far away from us is the Otherworld? Through what strange lands must Pwyll, Prince of Dyfed, ride in order to come into it? Over what strange seas, going ashore on what strange islands, must Bran Mac Feabhail voyage in order to find it?

If I were to meet old and wandering Aengus, if I were to meet him toiling through a hollow land or toiling up and down a hilly land, I'd greet him and I'd ask him to sit with me and I'd tell him a story.

There was an O'Malley man who lived at the foot of Oorid in Connemara. He one night dreamed that there was a great treasure hidden under O'Brien's Bridge in Limerick. Next morning, with the first light, he was on the road and two evenings later he was walking back and forth under the bridge seeing a clue to the treasure. Close by there was a cobbler working away inside the door of his little workshop. He saw the stranger and wondered what he was up to. He came out and he asked him if it was how he had lost something. 'No,' the O'Malley man said, ''tis how I dreamed that there was great treasure hidden here.' 'Isn't it a strange world,' the cobbler said, 'for though I'm not much given to dreaming, didn't I dream last night that there is a great treasure under a floor in Connemara. All I know is what the dream knows, that the house belongs to an O'Malley man and as far as I could pick it up and now remember tis under a hill called Oorid that he lives.'

Two evenings later, the O'Malley man lifted the biggest flag of his flagstone floor, and there it was.

So, Aengus, stop your wandering, go back to your floor, go back to your house. Maybe you remember it. It has a hazel wood at the back of it, it has a trout stream below it. It is where she has been waiting for you ever since she called you. So when you come over the brow of the last hill, don't be surprised to see smoke from your chimney and hens in the yard. It is to where we are that she calls us.

Stop your wandering, Aengus. And you, Bran, turn your ship round, for the Otherworld is a way of seeing this world. And the Otherworld well that the rivers of Ireland have their source in, that is everyone's well, it is your well, it is the well the least cherished of your slave girls dips her bucket into every morning.

There is of course a Christian way of putting all this. There are two Easters. There is an Easter in which we awaken to the extraordinary. There is an Easter in which we awaken to the ordinary. Of these two, the second is by far the more blessed.

Since the day we were born, and from long before we were born, the ordinary world has been calling us.

It is still calling us.

Tá sé ag glaoch orainn.
Tá sé ag glaoch orainn.
Tá sé ag glaoch orainn.

Run your finger through your hair, Aengus. Now smell them. They smell of hair, not of apple blossom. In your absence, though, she keeps the fire, she feeds the hens, she looks after the cattle. But, until you come home to your ordinary self, you cannot come home to her.

She is waiting.

Living where I now lived, with horses sometimes in the yard, with cats calling nightly at my door, I felt that I was an Aengus who had made it. I had come home.

Sounds there were, three sounds, that I would listen to.

The sound of my fire, its sods of black turf giving off yellow flames, its logs giving off white flames.

The sound of the river rushing through a rock cutting.

And the sound of the wind. In off the ocean, just in, it would sing its sea shanties, all of them lonesome, in the January trees.

It was difficult. A scaldcrow would pick out the eyes of a ewe in labour, and yet there were days when I couldn't go along with Vaughan's vision, not here in Connemara:

> I saw Eternity the other night
> Like a great Ring of pure and endless light,
> All calm, as it was bright,
> And round beneath it, Time in hours, days, years
> Driv'n by the spheres
> Like a vast shadow mov'd, In which the world
> And all her train were hurl'd ...

After a whole day in the silence of a corrie in the Maamturks, I'd come down into Glen Inagh and if Eternity would but stand where I stood and look on at the world it would hang its head, not in shame, but in slightly abashed wonder at this vision of itself.

No. There were evenings in Connemara when *world* didn't rhyme with *hurled*. Time, on such evenings, wasn't sundered into hours, days, years. It wasn't driven by the spheres. It was Eternity in a wonder of breathless self-awareness.

It was good not to have answers, not to know why we are in Eternity and yet exiled from it.

The best I could do was to live in a way that wouldn't shut out the sound of that stream coming down Eagle Mountain.

What I did know is that Bran will find what he seeks only when he turns his ship round and comes home.

A fear I had when I thought about quitting in Canada was how I would get on without the company, without the very presence and shape, of a woman. So far it wasn't an issue. And the reason wasn't far to seek. I was living a richly and splendidly sensuous life. Sensuous not just in my five senses. Sensuous in my mountain-climbing muscles. Sensuous in my bog-crossing, river-crossing, wood-sitting and wood-recumbent bones. Sensuous in my mind. In a mind as sensuous as my senses. Sensuous in my waking and in my sleeping. So in the way of the world, so of the world and so with the world was my bed, that to lie down into it was like lying down into the swan's nest, and so of the earth and so not of culture were my dreams, that I would sometimes wonder if the hare's form didn't every night grow back about my head, sheltering it in my sleep.

And I was wild.

Walking into snow flurries along a mountain ridge, along the rugged, quartzite ridge of Derryclare, I knew it. Having more mind to be wild with than they had, I was wilder than otter and heron. As well as being wild in my senses and instincts, I was philosophically wild. For how, living in Connemara, could I be an Aristotelian? How, living in Connemara, could I be a Platonist, a Thomist, a Rationalist, an English empiricist, a Hegelian, or, God bless us, a Positivist?

Philosophically, in Connemara, what else could I do but climb up out of Europe and say a Hindu hello to the clouds and the stars, and to the earth. Hindus looked about them and with a great, wide wave of the hand they said, all of this also is Brahman.

On a day when the mountains are blue, a deep, deep blue, because approaching cloud cover has softened the light, on such a day I'd know that I didn't go at all far enough when I said that matter is mind in hibernation. Something there is that is anterior to the miseries and sublimities and vulgarities of mind, and to day I only need to walk up into Glen Choaghan and it will be all around me.

If it was in Glen Choaghan today, the wonder of walking into Chartres Cathedral would be nothing to the wonder of walking out of it.

Connemara is dangerous, I would often think.

It dissolves myths.

It dissolves utterance.

But that doesn't mean that silence is good enough. If the silence is my silence, if it is me being silent, then it isn't good enough. Only being out of the way is good enough. But then, aware of the threat, my whole life would close like a fist into and around its identity and, the danger survived, I would come home.

Next day I'd be back and, climbing a hill, it wouldn't be from Leonardo's sketchbooks that I'd have knowledge of my leg muscles, my thigh muscles, my back muscles or my chest muscles. I would know them achingly, but, for all that, sensuously, and one day, as I climbed, I pictured myself sitting in an office in Winnipeg. There, on a typical day, I would be in touch mostly with manufactured things, with cups, with tables, with desks, a deadly blackboard behind me, function walls around me. Turning the walls of my apartment into a reproduced Renaissance, a reproduced Byzantium, a reproduced this, that and the other thing – it all helped of course, but in the end not a whole lot. In common with almost everyone else I knew, I suffered from sensuous, from somatically sensuous deprivation. Lacking the sensuousness of sitting for hours under a waterfall, of walking in high heather, of climbing a hill, of listening to a sheep-farmer talking in Irish about winters past and to come, I had a correspondingly greater need not to go home alone.

In Connemara there are other allurings, and it is always in pathless places, a hare or maybe a stoat distracting us onto it, that we once again pick up the trail.

After less than a year here, I knew how greatly we impoverish our lives when we assume that there is only one puberty, the sexual one. (*Nostos*, pp. 483–90)

The Everlasting Hymn of Praise & God I Am

(John Moriarty and Sacred Ritual)

John Moriarty reflected deeply on all aspects of life and culture. He was rightly appalled by the atrocities humans inflicted on fellow humans down the centuries from the Coliseum to Auschwitz. He declared: 'To stand in Auschwitz is to have your backbone turned into a question mark about the nature of the human being.' He concluded that no, we are not in fact anthropus *but* deinanthropus *(a word he himself coined). This is scary and would be totally disabling without divine assistance. John felt the remedy was in a great story and a great religion, like Christianity, that has its original and continuing source in the Triduum Sacrum – the three great days of Holy Thursday, Good Friday and Easter morning: 'In Jesus from*

Grand Canyon deep in it, from Good Friday deep in it, something in William James' phrase, was eternally gained for the universe. In Him the evolution of life on earth took its frightful final steps.' (Turtle *vol. 1, p. xxiv*)

John now realized Jesus is our Tirthankara who found the ford by which we can safely cross to the other shore. The ford is the Triduum Sacrum that brings newness of life in the very world we are born in, so we can travel on a road of imitations from the moment the paschal candle is set up by our cradle at baptism to the moment is set up by our coffin at the funeral rite.

John often reflected on a profoundly moving experience of ritual he had in his young life while kneeling in silent adoration before the Blessed Sacrament exposed in his parish church. Its lasting effects stayed with him his whole life long even when he became agnostic after reading Darwin's Origin of the Species in his teenage years.

In Connemara he was shattered back into prayer by a mystical experience at Lough Inagh. He spent a year in a Carmelite monastery under the direction of a Fr Norbert. John reflected: *'Just as nature has naturally selected metamorphosis in insects so can religion religiously select the most mystical of Rituals. This it does in Tenebrae.'* (Slí na Fírinne, *p. 126*). This ritual liturgically re-enacts what Jesus endured in the Triduum Sacrum when he went down through all the strata of the ages Grand Canyon deep in the world's karma and healed it all towards God. For John this Ritual of Tenebrae is adequate to all that we deinanthropically are. He believed that mediating the necessary graces to us, it enables us into and through our further and final evolution.

John was an innovator and he planned a Christian monastic hedge school for adults. He bought a plot of land on the hills outside Kilgarvan in Kerry and secured planning permission to build what he described as a New Temple for the era of Canyon Christianity. 'If, while I was in the womb, my umbilical cord had been cut, I would have been in trouble, wouldn't I? Similarly if my connection with the divine is severed, there is essential nourishment I am not getting and whether I acknowledge it or not I am in trouble – and a sense of trouble to whatever environs me.' (Turtle vol. 2, p. xxiii) He would call this new monastery Slí na Fírinne (Trail of Truth – the Adventure of our Immortality). Here one could live in baptismal assimilation to Christ. Tenebrae would be the chief ritual celebrated here, and for this John composed an entirely new text based largely on the writings of the Christian mystics, which he called the Bible of the Triduum Sacrum. (Turtle vol. 1, p. xiii)

John felt that what mystics suffered going through the dark night of the soul describes more adequately than the gospels do what Jesus suffered in his Passion and death. Performing Tenebrae in this new monastery one would keep watch with Jesus in Gethsemore and on Golgotha until his reappearance in the garden of the Sepulchre on Easter morning. This watching is not mere 'looking on' but is in fact a baptismal assimilation to Christ. With senses and faculties quenched like extinguished candles one is on the way to the cloud of unknowing. His hope was that what religion selects nature would in time select. Having become second nature, habit might in time become primary nature. (Slí na Fírinne, *p. 126)*

In this new monastery an equally important practice would be ephphata – the opening of the senses in places of outstanding beauty in nature. Here one could attain silver branch perception and with eyes and mind wide open one could be apocalypsed into the ordinary when the wonder child is alive and one comes home to where they are in their surroundings. Insight and consciousness happens there. This is the Paradise one lives in and it is then Easter morning in their nature now.

John was aware of how the Divine is always at work and how the genius of nature and of the universe is not static but dynamic and alive so that one could be surprised at any moment. All is in fact one and interconnected. The God of Surprises could manifest in any ordinary bush or tree for those with eyes to see and the universe could shine through the impairments of ones thinking about it. Open in instinct, eye and mind, one sees and experiences differently and sees all the way through to the very depths of reality where there is no object of awareness. Then going beyond mental activity one comes to Divine Ground.

One enters the All.

It happened to John.

It can happen to anyone.

It was Arthur Eddington who said, 'Something unknown is doing we don't know what.'

When palaeontologists began to seriously classify fossils they invariably denominated them by combining appropriate Greek words. So it was that they combined deinos and saurus, thus getting dinosaur, meaning terrible lizard.

The reality of who and what we are demanding it, it would be wise on our part were we to put deinos and anthropus together, thus getting the noun deinanthropus and the adjective deinanthropic, words suggesting immensities of biological and parabiological inwardness.

To migrate from an anthropic to a deinanthropic sense of ourselves – that from our first emergence has been the next evolutionary move or mutation that has awaited us.

Western history makes one thing profusely and prodigally evident: it is perfect folly to go on devising a culture for ourselves, to go on legislating for ourselves, on the obviously false assumption that we are anthropus, the truth being that we are deinanthropus.

In cultures not suited to us it is inevitable that what is deinanthropic in us will continue to blow up in our anthropic faces.

It's a dilemma.

For the reason we have suggested, it is perilous to live anthropically, to live in and from the more or less secure sense that inwardness is, by and large, the domain of ego, troublesome at times, but mostly manageable. It is on the other hand equally if not more perilous to live deinanthropically, to live, as so many mystics have, in full exposure to inner immensities, immensities into which and over which the ego's jurisdictive write does not run.

What to do? (*Slí na Fírinne*, p. 100)

*

What if we can be who we are,

>Deinanthropus?

Assuming that we can be, it is, I believe, a desirable ambition only within the providential care of a religion great enough to meet our need. That Christianity can be as great as we would deinanthropically need it to be I have no doubt. Let me say why.

To be deinanthropus is to be natively and almost infinitely available to immanence. It is to be natively and almost infinitely available to transcendence.

Now I speak of Jesus.

From the moment he crossed the Torrent, Jesus lived and was lived by this double availability as one simultaneous availability. Moreover, it was consciously, as microcosm, in Boehme's sense, that he lived and was lived by it. Saying the least we can say about this, it is the next big event in the evolution of our planet since the origin of DNA. And I can imagine nothing better for ourselves as we microcosmically are and for the earth in all its geological ages, past and to come, than that it would become encoded as a permanent evolutionary attainment in our DNA. A hope not so fantastic as it would at first sight seem when we think that metamorphosis has become genetically encoded in insects. Relevant here is something J.B.S. Haldane has said: 'It is my suspicion that the universe isn't only queerer than we suppose, it is queerer than we can suppose.'

Queer and improbable things can happen in it and to it. But, be that as it may.

Coming back from the liberalities of science fiction, there he is, Gerald Manley Hopkins telling us that man is no-man-fathomed man.

Listening to the Passion narratives, as Holderlin listened to Sophoclean tragedy, I think I hear, I am sure I hear, that man, in the gender inclusive sense, is being man-fathomed. A Christian, I think I hear, I am sure I hear, that man is being redemptively Godman-fathomed.

Let us look at ourselves.

Let us look at

Godman-fathomed humanity

Let us look at a wonder neither seen nor foreseen by the prophets and sybils of the Sistine ceiling, neither seen nor foreseen therefore by Renaissance humanism – let us look at

Deinanthropus

In the beginning, Goethe said, was the deed.

What Jesus undertook to do and undergo is, I believe, an originating deed. Given a chance, and with our good will, it would, I believe, generate a culture that would accommodate us as we have never previously been accommodated.

Wouldn't only accommodate us as an accomplished ontological fact of course. Would religiously and ritually accommodate us all the way into our further and final evolution. (*Slí na Fírinne*, p. 109–11)

*

Profoundest, most formative and most lasting education is in and by means of sacred ritual. In my own case it was what I experienced in church not what I learned in school that became destiny in me. Looking back on it now, my induction on to the Christian sacramental road from baptism to last rites is a supreme gift of my community to me. I well remember the day that Tom Callaghan, our teacher in primary school, sent Jim Stack and myself down to the parish church, not to clean it or any such thing, but to kneel in silent adoration of the most precious thing that mortal eyes could look upon, the consecrated Host, element of Christ's real presence among us, the holy thing right there, in radiant display at the windowed heart of a monstrance on the marble altar. As if the Host itself was radiating its divine glory, the monstrance was a rayed blaze of lunar silver. Later on, in another church, what I would see was a rayed blaze of solar gold. In time I would learn to sing a hymn called Panis Angelicus:

Panis angelicus, fit panis hominum, Dat panis caelicus figuris terminum, O res mirabilis ...

That was it, I had found the words for what Jim and myself had looked at. We had looked at and, in an utterly mysterious way, we had been divinely and lovingly looked at by, a *res mirabilis*, a thing yet more wonderful than a cowslip in the Hill Meadow when you got down on the ground and looked up into it.

And recently I asked, what is this *panis angelicus*, this bread, by which angels and archangels, by which the seraphim and the cherubim, are nurtured? Surely, I soon concluded, it is the ontologically resonant adoration evoked in them by their eternally beatifying vision of God. A vision mediated not just locally by their eyes but by all that they supernaturally are.

The Beatific Vision, that's it, that is what nurtures them, that is their bread. It is Isaiah who speaks:

> In the year that king Uzziah died I saw also the Lord sitting upon a throne, high and lifted up, and his train filled the temple. Above it stood the seraphims: each one had six wings; with twain he covered his face, and with twain he covered his feet, and with twain he did fly. And one cried unto another and said, Holy, holy, holy is the Lord of hosts: the whole earth is full of his glory.

There it is, the Song of the Angels, called the Kedushah in Hebrew, the Trishagion in Greek and the Sanctus in Latin, and every Sunday morning at Mass the celebrating priest invited us to fall in with them and sing it:

Et ideo cum Angelis et Archangelis, cum Thronis et Dominationibus, cumque omni Militia Caelestis exercitus, hymnum gloriae tuae canimus, sine fine dicentes, Sanctus, Sanctus, Sanctus, Dominus Deus Sabaoth, pleni sunt caeli et terra Gloria tua.

We who, an hour earlier would have been milking cows, feeding calves and pigs and turkeys and hens and getting out of our everyday clothes and getting into our Sunday clothes, and fighting over the shoe polish and over who was next at the water basin and next to stand before the mirror – us, a squabble of ordinary people falling reverently silent as we enter the church, and soon there we are, not singing a Come All Ye in a pub, but singing their Kedushah with angels, a few of whom we knew by name, Uriel, Gabriel, Michael, Raphael, and what's more, our eyes aren't covered, as theirs are, with wings, or with our cow-milking, pig-feeding hands.

Also, I remember my confirmation. Looking like he had walked out of a holy picture, the bishop finally came to me. Laying his left hand on my head, he dipped his thumb into the chrismary and then making the sign of the cross on my forehead with the chrism he said:

Signo te signo crucis et confirmo te Chrismate salutis. In nomine Patris et Filii et Spiritui Sancti. Amen.

Striking me gently on the cheek, he said:

Pax tecum.

In English it reads: I sign you with the sign of the cross and I confirm you with the chrism of salvation. In the name of the Father and the Son and the Holy Spirit. Amen.

Peace be with you.

At that moment the heavens opened above me and everything that happened to the Apostles on Pentecost Sunday, that and more happened to me. I was Pentecosted. The seven gifts of the Holy Ghost came down into me and for over a year now, as part of my preparation for their descent upon me, I knew them by heart. They were wisdom, understanding, counsel, fortitude, knowledge, piety and fear of the Lord. And yet something more. What I was assured of beforehand but could hardly credit was that I had become a temple of the Holy Ghost. More than anything else though, what I would remember was the half an hour I spent with Jim Stack, two lads on furlough from genitives and fractions, kneeling in silent adoration before the blaze of lunar silver and the res mirabilis that it housed. Again and again I would go back to it in my mind and even when I had ceased to be a Christian I'd re-enter that church, I'd kneel where I knelt, hoping for irradiation by it. (*What the Curlew Said*, pp. 319–21)

*

A sacrament, we were taught in school, is a visible enactment by which an invisible grace is conferred. In that sense of it, the Christian sacramental road is a great road or, should I say, in my experience of it, it is a great road, and I am happy that I found my way back to it.

People interested in such matters talk about a dual literary tradition in Ireland, one in Gaelic, the other in English. Like others of my education and age, however, I grew up in a triune linguistic tradition, of English, Gaelic and Church Latin, and because of its constant association with liturgy, because of its liturgical radiance, Church Latin is the one that has most deeply destined me. From the heart of the terrible, from the heart of the sometimes crucifying world, it calls out:

Sursum Corda.

What I haven't got used to, even in liturgical Latin, is the fact that Jesus put bloodshed at the heart of our dealings with God and put His sacramentally edible flesh and sacramentally drinkable blood at the heart our dealings with Himself. From all of which I have moved on, downward into Canyon Christianity. The second coming of Christ is a mystical understanding of the first.

Time was when we believed that our God was angry with us over our many failings, the first of them a transmitted sin committed by our first parents in Paradise. Down the generations, we needed to appease God and to expiate our sin in its original form and in all subsequent instances and repetitions of it. In quite a terrible way, Jesus engaged with us in both needs. He did so to the point of exoneration and redemption.

But Jesus isn't only scapegoat:

And Aaron shall lay both his hands upon the head of the live goat, and confess over him all the iniquities of the children of Israel, and all their transgressions in all their sins, putting them upon the head of the goat, and shall send him away by the hand of a fit man into the wilderness: And the goat shall bear upon him all their iniquities unto a land not inhabited: and he shall let go the goat in the wilderness.

I think of Jesus in that same wilderness. One day He sees a shimmer in the heat haze. Turning aside, He sees that it is last year's scapegoat. Not knowing how or why, He senses a moment of destiny. Thinking about it, He concludes that, no, we shouldn't lay the burden of human sin and guilt on an animal. Only on a conscious human being consciously choosing to be the victim. Even if it was something in human beings themselves, not God, that needed to be appeased, so be it. Once and for all, sometime soon, He would lay Himself open to what He knew would be real devastation. It is a choice that many have difficulty with. But the thing about Jesus is that, no matter what the situation, He was never tempted to choose either a detour or a short cut. Born as He was in a stable, He would relate to us not just ideally but as and how He found us.

But Jesus isn't only the Lamb of God:

Lamb of God, you who take away the sins of the world,
    have mercy on us.
Lamb of God, you who take away the sins of the world,
    have mercy on us.
Lamb of God, you who take away the sins of the world,
    grant us peace.

In a way but barely imaginable, Jesus is pioneer. Having gone down into a depth within Himself where 'I' is 'we' and having endured us back into God, Jesus is Tirthankara, He is the opener of a way for all things in all geological ages.

No, Jesus isn't only an archetype, a scapegoat hung up to die in a drama of appeasement and expiation in the wilderness of Calvary. Tremendously, immensely, resplendently, He is neotype, He is teleotype, and as such He needs a new a new Bible all to Himself. Interesting in this regard is the fact that Mallarme was of the opinion that our age is seeking to bring forth a new holy book. I think of it as a book about Christ in the Canyon. And so, if someone else doesn't do it, I will. Making the sign of the cross upon myself, I announce a new Christian epoch, the epoch of Canyon Christianity, the epoch in which we know that Jesus is still at work, still claiming the whole Canyon for culture, the whole psyche for sanctity, the epoch in which Bright Angel Trail is ambulatory, the epoch of final adaptation, the epoch in which we adapt to ourselves as potential jivanmuktas and to the Earth as Buddh Gaia.

Having all of this in mind, I formulated a Nicene Creed for myself. In it I attend not to who Jesus is but to what He undertook and achieved.

> The Jesus we come to know in the Gospels isn't the whole story. He has continued and will continue to grow in human consciousness. He grows in accordance with our need and in accordance with our ability and willingness

to welcome Him in this His further growing. And so it is that for Him neither Christmas nor Ascension Thursday are biographical bounding walls.

In His role as scapegoat, Jesus crosses the Torrent into the Garden of Olives, He goes on to an expiating death by crucifixion on Calvary and two mornings later He reappears among us in the Garden of the Sepulchre. As pioneer, He crosses the Torrent into Gethsemane, that the very deep place of the mirroring rock pool, and from there He climbs a Canyon mesa called Golgotha or the Metanoetic Nunatak, both names telling us that it rises above dualizing mind, both names telling us that as well as being a height it is a depth, in the end a nowhere, in which we endure the dreadful but blessed and beatifying mortifications of the dark night of the soul. Jesus carried His Cross to a height and a depth called Golgotha.

It was consciously as microcosm that Jesus did what He did and endured what He endured in the Canyon. Commensurate with this are such consequences as

Gaiakhty
and
Buddh Gaia.

Comensurate with it is a brightened galaxy.
Commensurate with the is astronomical optimism.
In regard to final evolutionary transitions what is true of the microcosm is true of the macrocosm. (*What the Curlew Said*, pp. 319–24)

*

I baptize you.

I absolve you.

I confirm you with the chrism of salvation.

May perpetual light shine upon you,
may you rest in peace.

A far cry, these sounds, from what for Christians are the sounds of the universe turning, as it were upon its axle, back into God:

the drip drip drip drop drop drop drop of water into wine, and the sound of dry, wafer-thin bread being broken.

And something else. In Passiontide, in Holy Week, on Holy Thursday night or on the night maybe of Good Friday, the monks whose church this was would have set up the Tenebrae harrow in the sanctuary. A triangular candelabrum set on a tall standard, the harrow had seven candles on each ascending side and one at the apex. Over hours they would chant the great tragic Psalms, long extracts from the Lamentations of Jeremiah and a Passion Narrative, all this and more. Concurrently with this, at set intervals, a candle would be quenched and this would go on until only the candle at the apex was still lighting. Finally, this, the light of

Christ, was taken down and carried round and entombed behind the altar. And so it was that they had let the very particular darkness of Good Friday, called Tenebrae, come upon them. So it was that they had let the Darkness of God come upon them. And likely it is that there will have been a monk or two who won't only have walked beside Jesus. Their baptism still active in them, they will have walked in sacramental assimilation to him, enduring his dreadful night and his yet more dreadful noon with him.

Candles quenched and, as though they were distractions, our senses and faculties quenched. As quenched as they are in dream-less sleep. Out of God's way now, what may happen next Meister Eckhart has described:

> Comes then the soul into the unclouded light of God. It is transported so far from creaturehood into nothingness that, of its own powers, it can never return to its senses and faculties or its former creaturehood. Once there, God shelters the soul's nothingness with his uncreated essence, safeguarding its creaturely existence. The soul has dared to become nothing, and cannot pass from its own being into nothingness and back again, losing its own identity in the process, except God safeguarded it. This must needs be so.

Here we are back to what his God said to Al Niffari, a great Muslim mystic:

> Between Me and thee is thy self-experience. Cast it from thee and I will veil thee from thyself.

The difference between Inisfree and Inisfallen is that here, on Inisfallen, there is a church. Here there is what Philip Larkin would call a serious house on serious earth, a house in which, he would say, it is proper to grow wise in. In this house we more wisely and therefore more safely lay ourselves open to the blessed devastation of the stroke of midnight:

> At stroke of midnight soul cannot endure
> A bodily or a mental furniture.

There is our natural genome and there is the Christian genome of sacraments such as Baptism and of rituals such as Tenebrae.

Our Christian genome takes us into and through a sequence of astounding transitions the blueprints for which are not to be found in our natural genome. Think of our final transition as Eckhart has described it and we see that what the Christian genome has in mind is our further and final evolution. Our evolution, in the end, from that in us which evolves.

Observing the way in which custom can become second nature, Pascal wondered whether nature itself is but a first custom. Assuming for the moment that this is so, it mightn't be entirely fantastical in a sci-fi way to imagine that our Christian and our natural genomes might one day merge, this meaning that our further and final evolution would then be genetically encoded, this meaning, that in merging with it, second nature would become primary nature.

All in all, I disagree with Nietzsche when he says that Christianity is the greatest calamity that has so far afflicted humanity. And I will not be putting my shoulder to the cannon-carriage wheel of one of Voltaire's revolutionary ambitions expressed as an incitement to destruction in two words:

> *Ecrasez l'infame.*
> Destroy the infamy.

The Chinese have it that the sage will more often than not be found walking, not ahead of humanity, pioneering a way for it, but behind it, picking up the wonderful things it leaves behind it in its flight into a future that might well turn out to be what so many of our futures have been, costly failures.

Starting in the early autumn and continuing into winter, the ice cap spreads south from the polar regions. Seals caught up in this advance have to keep breathing-holes open in the ice. After a fifteen-minute dive or so, seeking for food, they must come up in to these breathing-holes and draw breath in them. It is what the Christian sacraments are, I sometimes think: seals' breathing-holes in which we breathe transcendentally. Without such breathing something essential to our humanity dies, or rather, something essential to our humanity doesn't come to life.

Here, right here, is a theory of culture.

Here, right here, we are back in dialogue with Plato and St Augustine. (*Serious Sounds*, pp. 58–62)

*

Believing that it will help us to cross the Torrent with Jesus, we listen to the Mandukya Upanishad in Christian translation.

THE MANDUKYA UPANISHAD
A CHRISTIAN TRANSLATION

Why else except in the hope of sanctity would I continue to live, I one day asked myself, and with that I walked out and walked up along our river, all the way up to its headwaters and it's here, in a herd's house, that I have lived ever since.

The perversity of it, I thought. To be born for conversation and to have no one to converse with. To be the kind of man that a woman would fall for and here I was, higher than cowslips and grouse, going to bed alone.

Some mornings the mountains were numerously murderous. Put a foot wrong up there on one of those ridges and all the way down along a jagged fall you'd be hung up in morsels convenient for carrion crows. And worse altogether it would be, up here, to put a foot wrong inside of your mind.

Other mornings, trusting to what your eyes saw not to what your mind knew, you'd be tempted to set out and walk through these same mountains, thinking them to be accumulations and shapes of pure blue soul.

On such mornings to impute meaning to the world was to impugn the world. I called all meanings home, and that was the most dangerous and the most reckless thing I had so far done in my life.

It was a shock to discover how infested with meanings my eyes and mind had been.

Not eclipsed by meaning, the January moon brightened my yard with a light not sheathed in adverb or adjective.

Shining, but not through our astronomies, the stars would some nights look like they had it in for the Earth. Even in my water-butt, water that mirrored them had a wounded taste.

It was tough going, fasting not from this or that minor instinct, fasting from a chief instinct, our instinct to meaning.

Having no mirror, I could only imagine how emaciated my eyes and mind looked.

Going to bed at night, knowing that it was ahead of me anyway, I would willingly surrender to dreamless sleep, meaning that I was willing to forfeit all sense of my own existence, meaning that I was willing to give up being me, to give up being anything at all, to give up being.

Meditating three times a day, I would seek to be as ascetic awake as I was in dreamless sleep. Achingly, I had an anaesthetic sense that in such anaesthetic self-abeyance I was next door to God. More. I was available to take-over by God.

Awake, the self-abeyance was never complete. Self couldn't dissolve self. The best I could do was to turn the work over to God. My part was to be annihilatingly available.

It was how I understood the horror of Jesus on Golgotha.

It was in baptismal assimilation to him that I continued.

When it came, inwardly and outwardly the catastrophe was ragnarok big. In an instant, long as forever, I underwent utter disillusionment, compelling me to inherit a Hindu estimation of mind and world. It was like waking up in and within dreamless sleep: mind as source of the world-illusion and the world illusion itself, both were gone, and I was a terrorized trembling in the nothingness.

It was ruination of a kind that I couldn't have anticipated. And even if they were Siberian shamans or Viennese psychoanalysts, there was no point in calling the king's horses, no point in calling the king's men.

Soon there was something else I came to know. There is in the human body a physical appendix into which its poisons drain. Similarly, there is in the human psyche a karmic appendix and in me now it had burst, flooding my mind, fogging my eyes, my room, my windows. What was so ruinously frightful was that the horror-images were impulse-images.

They were impulsions to action.

Naively, I gave myself a year to come through. Seventeen years later, out of the blue, it would be as though I had drunk the wine of astonishment, as though I had yet again drained the dregs of the cup of trembling.

Sometimes I would ask myself, must nearness to God mean ruination? Is that what Golgotha means?

I would think of Jesus, his head collapsed onto his chest, his meaningless eyes looking down into his own empty skull.

Fantastically, I would dare to believe that Golgotha isn't exaggeration. The Passion from beginning to end isn't exaggeration.

Christ in Gethsemane, Christ on Golgotha, Christ in the Garden of the Sepulchre, how surprised I was that all of this made sense to me. How surprised I was at how soon it became visual vocabulary to me.

Just my luck to find myself baptismally reassimilated to Christ in his Passion, that at a time when, chiefly perhaps because of its scenic horror, people were walking out of it.

Stellar astronomy.
Starless astronomy.

   The starless astronomy of Good Friday.

   The blessed catastrophe of the empty skull.

   It is worth it.

   Days there are.

Up here, higher than primroses and grouse, but not always higher than hell, it is what I mean by making the sign of the cross on myself.

   Shantih   Shantih   Shantih

   (*Slí na Fírinne*, pp. 77–9)

A Walkabout in Dreamtime Ireland

*John Moriarty diagnosed modern culture in trouble because of the damage being done to the universe. He believed we could have a more adequate life in Ireland today by calling it into an image or archetype of itself through a safari of stories (*Invoking Ireland*, p. 8). He felt poets could do this by healing our cultural past so a healed present could grow. (*Dreamtime*, p. viii)*

John himself walked the old song lines telling stories from every province in Ireland. To walk with him we must leave our modern mind with its Western education behind and feel instead what Yeats felt: a fire in the head as we enter the hazel wood, which is really a place inside the mind below all our learning in logic and science. It is below the discursive ways of thinking we learned.

We need to go right down to 'the deep hearts core' that education knows nothing about. We come to that part of the human psyche and the psyche of the universe that knows the little silver trout can instantly turn into a girl with apple blossom in her hair. (Slí na Fírinne, p. 53)

Going into the hazel wood we cross a threshold out of our modern European state of mind and we enter the Otherworld where reality behaves differently from what we are accustomed to. To illustrate this, John loved to quote an Inuit Eskimo of the Polar North:

> *In the very earliest time when both people and animals lived on earth a person could become an animal if he wanted to and an animal could become a human being. Sometimes they were people and sometimes animals, and there was no difference. All spoke the same language. That was the time when words were like magic. The human mind had mysterious powers. A word spoken by chance might have strange consequences. It would suddenly come alive and what people wanted to happen could happen – all you had to do was say it. Nobody can explain this: that's the way it was.* (Slí na Fírinne, p. 48)

John was adamant we too could discover this at some level of our mind if we go on an exodus from Newton and $E=MC^2$ to the dimension of the universe that exists in an 'elsewhere', in once-upon-a-time.

We can do this by invoking the blessing of the Aes Sídhe – the divine powers in the landscape hidden from ordinary sight. These would introduce us to the eternal ones of the dream – our ancestors like Fintan Mac Bochra (Fintan, Son of the Sea) who came to Ireland before the biblical flood, or Bran Mac Feabhail who met Manannán (God of the Sea).

To be able for this learning it is essential to break down the Hadrian's Wall inside our own mind that cuts us off from the Shamanic North. Then the 'wonder eye' can open in us and *we can commune with birds and animals and be in tune with Earth's rhythms as we feel the genius and magic of the world.*

*Instead of looking south to the Mediterranean for culture we look to the Shamanic North to see what we have blocked out and lost. We develop a new form of mind cultivated by myths that put us in touch with the powers of the Otherworld at levels and depths of our own psyche. We leave the world of Descartes and join Yeats who maintains that all vision and insight begins with dreams and that for each person there is one scene or one image that leads them to wisdom to live by. William James calls this the wisdom of 'immediate luminousness', intuited by the heart and the senses and the imagination, expressed in stories, myths and poetry that generate awe and wonder, deeper than thought. (*Nostos*, p. 9)*

*John Moriarty had a genome of stories that are culturally genetic to the Irish. If we listen to them we can be generated culturally in instinct eye and mind and be enabled to live poetically on the land. (*Invoking Ireland, *p. 15)*

*These stories resist linearity. Instead, they are a tapestry of themes and styles. The hope is when one comes to the end and stand back a unified picture does in fact emerge. (*Dreamtime, *p. ix)*

*These stories cross the Kedron with Jesus and stand Grand Canyon deep in the world's karma giving us Second Coming Christianity by which we can travel on a Christian Sacramental road. (*Invoking Ireland, *p. 13)*

All this could heal our civilization for what the unconscious is to consciousness, Ireland's Dreamtime is to Ireland's history. Putting the new intelligence on display, we need a particular way to be alert and awake. We too can become Olamh Fódhla and we can come out of the anaesthetic and come to a plenitude of Being in a plenary world. (Slí na Fírinne, *p 48*)

CES NOIDHEN

Towards the end of the last century, Yeats and Lady Gregory spent many days together collecting folklore in the countryside around Coole in the west of Ireland. In the course of their work they discovered that

> When we passed the door of some peasant's cottage we passed out of Europe as that word is understood.

The Europe they here have in mind is of course official Europe, the Europe that continues to have its cultural origins in Hebrew prophecy, Greek philosophy and science, and Roman law.

And now at last a door, and we lift the latch, and the voice that says come in could be the voice of Fintan Mac Bóchra. It could be the voice of Merlin or Taliesin. It could be the voice of Morgan le Fay.

And how strange it is to stumble on the path that takes us to that door. And how strange it is to lift that latch. And how strange it is to hear that voice. And how strange it is to discover we were always so near home.

Coming again the next day, that path might not be there.

There, but not there for us.

Not there for us because now again we have no eyes for it.

Our eyes are for seeing hard facts.

Hadrian's Wall is a hard fact.

First, it fenced us into a world of hard facts.

Now, stronger than ever, it fences us into a world of manufactured hard facts, it fences us into official Europe. And we don't even wail at it. Nor do we take a sledge to it. It is within a great prison we are unconscious of that we celebrate our Bastille Day.

Almost from the beginning, the wall that Hadrian had built across the north of England became an inner wall. A defensive wall, it has served its sundering purpose only too well, and we, its prisoners, we have gone on building it, deepening it, widening it, filling up cracks in it. Fortunately no crack was wide enough, not even the crack we call Romanticism was wide enough, to let Merlin walk through.

From before a foundation stone of it was laid, Aristotle had a hand in it. More recently, Descartes had a hand in it. On a morning when he celebrated Christ's nativity, Milton had a hand in it, forced his Saviour, infant though he was, to have a dredded hand in it. Locke had a hand in it. Indeed, all rationalist and empirical philosophers had a hand in it. Hardly an eighteenth- or nineteenth-century scientist but had a hand in it.

We have gone on building your wall for you, Hadrian. Building it inwardly and outwardly against shamanic Eurasia. Building it inwardly and outwardly against Faerie. Building it inwardly and outwardly against our Dreamtime.

Against Merlin, Taliesin and Morgan le Fay.
Against Boann, Badb and Cailleach Beara.
Against Ollamh Fódhla.
Against Fintan Mac Bóchra.
Against Pwyll, Prince of Dyfed.

It wasn't by sitting at home, waiting for a turn in the weather, that Pwyll came to know where a stag hunt might lead if it led to Glen Cuch.

It wasn't by sitting at home, waiting for the spring run of salmon in the river, that Pwyll found the crone and the crone found the well where he slept for nine nights, on nine hazel wattles, seeking a vision his people could live by.

It wasn't by sitting at home, waiting till his minstrel had come to the end of his winter cycle of stories, that Pwyll rode back one day, his banner of lordship in the Otherworld streaming behind him.

Pwyll in our world meant the heraldry of the Otherworld in our world. Streaming from tower and outer wall, they would brighten a sad day in Dyfed.

It was the time of year when Pwyll and his men-at-arms rode to his court in Arberth. The sun picking out great braveries of armour and ornament, they rode four abreast and, to a man, they had the look of men who lived in hillforts and worshipped in henges.

Theirs was a world that had genius in every stone and bush of it, and it wasn't by incantation that a bush would enchant you, leaving you helpless, your hand halt, and your sword hanging idle at your thigh. Rough men though they were, and intent on adventure, not one of them but knew when to rein in his horse. Riding together or alone, riding at nightfall in desolate places, not one of them but knew when to rein in his instincts.

It was that kind of world. A man who had won everlasting renown in a long war might die coming home when a hare who wasn't a hare of this world put an eye that wasn't an eye of this world upon him. Upon him and his horse.

To die in circumstances such as these was, more often than not, to be called away to a glorious life in a glorious elsewhere. Of such a man his companions and neighbours would say that he had been swept. By whom they would, in awful reverence, rarely say. Any yet everyone knew that it was the Aes Shidhe.

The world he had gone into wasn't far away. Nights there would be when people would hear overhead the hosts of the air go riding by and someone who had second sight would recognize the dead man, glorious now on a glorious steed, riding among them. And it was well known that a woman who loved a swept man could, in a ritual performed at a crossroads, induce him or even compel him to come back.

It was that kind of world.

It was a world of worlds, all of them one world, all of them a world in which there was coming and going between worlds.

As often as not, Pwyll Prince of Dyfed was called Pwyll Pen Annwn, Pwyll who was Head of the Otherworld.

Like all of us, although in our case at an unknown or unrecognized depth of ourselves, Pwyll was a Lord in two worlds. Had the banners of two worlds flying from his towers.

Every year, at leaf-fall, Pwyll and his men rode to Arberth. Riding through a valley five valleys from home they were like an old story Taliesin would tell. And they had it in them to go with the story. They had it in them, living now, riding now to Arberth, to be a tale told by a fireside in the far past, to be a tale told by a fireside in the far future. And they would say, would sometimes say, that their only reason for being in the world was to give the world a chance to live out its own strangeness, its own danger, and its own wonder in them. And this year, reaching Arberth, that's what they looked like. They looked like men who had survived. They looked like men who had come through a dream that Ceridwen, having drunk a new brew from her cauldron, had of them. After meat and good cheer in his hall the next day, Pwyll announced, as though something had come over him, that he would now go out and sit on the throne mound. At his bidding, a score of men, and they the bravest, accompanied him.

Famous in all worlds, even in worlds we rarely cross into, the throne mound in Dyfed was called Gorsedd Arberth. A thing of crags and swards, of furze and whitethorns, it was lair to a man's own fear of it. It was lair to his fear of himself. In some of its moods, horses, in screeching refusal, would rear at it. And so, it wasn't in ignorance of its perils that Pwyll climbed it. Today, sitting there, he knew that one or another of two adventures would befall him: either he would endure wounds and blows or he would see a wonder.

It was Teyrnon Twyrf Liant, Lord of Gwent Is Coed, who first saw it: in fields all about them not a horse but had stopped grazing and was looking intently, as if in a trance, towards the wood.

Pwyll was of the impression that they were looking into a depth of themselves and into a depth of the world that only the most privileged of us have ever walked in.

Persons so privileged, Pwyll was aware, had rarely come back.

Although he could never afterwards say how or why, Pwyll had come back, a pennant and banner of the Otherworld streaming above him in the January wind. And as he once came home having slept for nine nights on the nine hazel wattles, so now he came home with a boon for his people. He had news for his people: the Otherworld is a way of seeing this world, it is a way of being in this world. (*Dreamtime*, pp. 3–6)

*

Fintan mac Bochra

The geography of my mind is the geography of the world I walk in. In the geography of my mind and therefore also in the geography of the world I walk in are Sidh ar Feimhin, Linn Feic, Dá Chích na Morrigna and Connla's Well. And if you ask me about life, about what we haven't eyes for in this life, I will talk to you about Da. Chich na Morrigna and the paths to Sidh ar Feimhin. And the stars, if you ask me about the stars I will tell you that only they who have seen them mirrored in Linn Feic have knowledge of them, only they who have seen them mirrored in that divine deep within themselves can call themselves astronomers. And Connla's Well, at Connla's Other-world well it was I first realized that being human is a habit. It can be broken. Like the habit of going down to the river by this path rather than that, I broke it. And so it is that, although I always know who I am, I can never be sure that what I am going to sleep at night is what I will be when I wake up in the morning. In me the shape-shifts of sleep survive into waking. What I'm saying is, my shape depends on my mood. In one mood, as you can see, I'm an old man, old in the way weather-lore is old, old in the way old stories are old. In another mood I'm a salmon in Lough Derg. In a mood that lasted from the coming of Partholon to the coming of the Milesians I was a hawk in Achill.

Yes, that's how it is. You only need to break the habit once, the habit of being human I mean, and then you will be as you were between death and rebirth. Between death and rebirth our bodies are mind-bodies, and that means they are alterable. Alterable at will. We only have to will it and it happens, we flow from being a swan in Lough Owel into being a hind on Slieve Bloom into being a hare on Beara.

If for some reason he crosses into our world, the hare will have one red ear.

That's how it is.

What's possible for all of us there is possible for some of us here.

Mostly, though, we've forgotten all this, but folktales remember. Folktales aren't afraid. On its way to the well at the world's end, a folktale will stop by a rock and tell you that every seventh year, at Samhain, it turns into an old woman driving a cow. On its way to Linn Feic, a folktale will sit with you under a bush and, where a bard might tell you the history of your people awake, that bush will tell you the much more serious history of your people asleep.

And the folktale knows what so many people no longer know. It knows how to walk the path to Connla's Well. On the way to Connla's Well the world has shaken off the habit of being worldly. On the way to Connla's Well we come to see that the world's habit of being worldly is not in the world, it is in our eyes.

> As the folktale sees I see.
> As the folktale lives I live.
> And the path to my door, that too is folktale.
> Coming here, you either undergo what people undergo in a folktale or you'll never lift my latch.

> Little wonder I so rarely hear my latch being lifted.
> Little wonder I so rarely hear my latch being lifted.
> Little wonder I so rarely hear my latch being lifted.
> (*Invoking Ireland*, pp. 39–40)

*

Ollamh Fódhla

As is the case with all other rivers, our river has its source in Connla's Well. And that is why we learn to speak. For us, to learn to speak is to learn to say:

> Our river has its source in the Otherworld Well.

And anything we say about the hills and anything we say about the stars is a way of saying:

A hazel grows over the Otherworld Well our river has its source in.

Our time being so other than Otherworld time, it isn't often, in our time, that a hazel nut falls into Connla's Well, but when it does it is carried downstream and if, passing from current to current, it is brought to your feet and you eat it, then though in no way altered, sight in you will be pure wonder. Then, seeing ordinary things in the ordinary way you had always seen them, sight in you will be more visionary than vision.

To know, and to continue to know, that any well we dip our buckets into is Connla's Well is why we are a people.

We are a river people.

Exile for us is to live in a house that isn't river-mirrored. Our river isn't only a river. It is also the moon-white cow who will sometimes walk towards us, but not all the way to-wards us, on one or another of its banks.

The river and the cow we call by the same name. We call them Boann.

Boann, the moon-white cow.
Boann, the gleaming river.
In dreams I know it as cow.
Awake I know it as river.

And my house isn't only river-mirrored. It is mirrored in Linn Feic, its most sacred pool. And this is so because, by difficult and resisted destiny, I am ollamh to my people. They call me Ollamh Fódhla. In their view of me, Boann, the gleaming river, has carried a hazel nut to my feet.

As these things often do, it began in sleep, in dreams in the night: standing in my door I'd be tempted to think he was only a short morning's walk away, and yet it would often be nightfall before I'd at last turn back, not having made it. A sense I had is that the man I was seeking to reach was myself as I one day would be. In the most frightening of all the dreams I dreamed at that time a man who had no face came towards me and said, 'You are worlds away from him.' When he next came towards me he had a face and he said, 'You are as far away from him as waking is from dreaming.' In the end it was my own voice, more anguished. than angry, that I heard: it isn't distance, measurable in hours or days of walking, that separates you from what you would be. It is states of mind, yours more than his.

Defeated, I settled back into my old ways. At this time of year that meant that one morning I'd pull my door shut behind me and drive my cattle to the high grazing ground between the Paps of Morrigu.

My father who quoted his father had always assured me that there was no sacrilege in this. According to the oldest ancestor we had hearsay of, it was in no sense a right that we claimed. Fearfully, it was a seasonal rite we were called upon to undergo. This I took on trust, allowing that there was something more than good husbandry at stake.

Up here, summer after summer since I was a boy, we shook off the vexations and the weariness of winter enclosure.

Up here the gods were not fenced in.

Up here, when we heard him neighing, we knew that the horse god couldn't be cut down to cult size, couldn't be made to serve religious need.

Up here there is a rock. It so challenges our sane sense of things that I long ago capitulated to the embarrassment of crediting what my father and his father before him used to say about it, that every seven years, at Samhain, it turns into an old woman driving a cow.

Sensing my difficulties, my father was blunt: if in the eyes of the world you aren't embarrassed by your beliefs about the world then you may conclude that the wonder-eye that is in all of us hasn't yet opened in you.

That's how it was with me in those days. No sooner had I learned the world and learned my way in it than, standing in front of a rock or a tree, I'd have to unlearn it. I'd hear a story and think that's it, that's how the world is, that story will house me, but then there she'd be, the old woman driving her cow in through my front door and out through my back door, leaving me homeless yet again.

And it wasn't just anywhere I was homeless. I was homeless on the high grazing ground between the Paps of Morrigu, and it wasn't by hearsay that, however red-mouthed she was, Morrigu was divine, all the more divine in my eyes because, like the horse god who neighed only at night, she would never submit to religious servility. Though a people prayed to her she wouldn't send rain in a time of drought or stand in battle with them against an invader.

Worship of Morrigu, of red-mouthed Morrigu, had to be pure.

And that's what I did up here.

Up here every summer I lived between the breasts of a goddess who, in her form as scald crow, called above me every day, circled and called, searching for afterbirths, searching for corpses, searching for carrion.

The contradiction ploughed me. It ploughed me and harrowed me. 'Twas as if the breasts of the mother goddess had become the Paps of the battle goddess. And to live between the Paps was to live in trepidation of the divine embrace.

Sometimes hearing her call as a scald crow calls I would hear a demand: you must be religious but in being religious you must have no recourse to religion.

So that is it, I thought. That is the seasonal rite. To be religious here is to fast from religion.

These were heights I wasn't continuously able for. Always by summer's end I'd have lost my nerve, and now again I would pull a door shut behind me and I would go down, me and my cattle, my cattle going down to the shelter of the woods and swards along the river, and I going down to the shelter of traditional religion and story.

Here, as well as being a moon-white cow, the goddess is Boann, the gleaming river.

Down here, we are river-mirrored. And since it is the same sacred river that mirrors us, we are a people.

My house is mirrored in Linn Feic.

In a sense therefore I sleep in Linn Feic, I dream in Linn Feic.

At a sleeping depth of me that I'm not aware of, maybe I am a salmon in Linn Feic, and maybe I swim upstream every night, all the way up into the Otherworld, all the way up into Nectan's Well. At that depth of myself, maybe the shadows of the Otherworld hazel are always upon me. Are always upon all of us, letting wisdom and wonder drop down into us.

Could it be that we are safer in, our depths than we are in our heights? Or could it be that we will only be safe in our heights when we already know that we are safe in our depths?

This time the old woman didn't drive her cow through the conclusion I came to. This time, bringing a six years' solitude in the Loughcrew Hills to a sudden end, it was like a stroke, it was like waking up from waking. During an endless instant, all heights and depths had disappeared, leaving only a void, or what seemed like a void.

Twenty-six years later, sitting in my house by Linn Feic, I was able to say, it is in Divine Ground behind all depths and heights that we are safe.

That summer, sitting in my reconstructed but between the Paps, I was able to say, it is from Divine Ground behind and within them that we become able for our depths and heights.

Coming down, at a turn on the path where I was only a short morning's walk away from them, I felt I was able for the sense that people had of me. I felt I was able to be their ollamh. Opening my door, knowing that I was mirrored by the sacred river, I felt that in that depth of me that is overarched by the Otherworld hazel I had consented to be Ollamh Fódhla. (*Invoking Ireland*, pp. 41–5)

*

CONNLA'S WELL
None of my friends knew that during all those years I was in Otherworld fosterage to Connla.

I cut turf with them. I milked cows. I ground corn. I played hurling, coming off the bawn sometimes as badly bruised as the toughest of them.

What I didn't know and what they didn't know is that this world and the Otherworld are one world. How we perceive and live in this one world is what makes the difference. The Otherworld is a way of hearing and seeing.

I would often wake at dawn and I'd lie there listening to herring gulls and herons and curlews down on the shore.

There was a big heronry, sometimes more than twenty nests, in the wood behind our house. Under it, the floor of the wood was white with their scour. In spring, the smell of it would almost knock me, but I'd brave it anyway, for I loved to collect the turquoise shells or half shells they'd drop from their nests. The shell of herons' eggs were the only turquoise things in our world. Although sometimes, on a clear morning, the inlet of sea below our house, that too would be turquoise. But I couldn't collect that. A wind would be rising soon or the tide would ebb and I'd watch it fade.

How often I heard it, the screech and the croak of a heron flying over our house to her young at dawn.

A screech, a screech, a screech, a squabble of croaks, a dull croak. Herons flying over our house to their nests.

The giving and the lurid, loud greed of those early disgorgings. That's what I'd hear lying awake before dawn under our thatch. One of them is king, my father said. One of them is the king heron. He's the one with the sea-blue voice.

Pigs, they used to say, can see the wind. Can my father see sound? I wondered. I asked him.

Yes, he said. It's like lightning and thunder. First I see the lightning and then, waiting awhile, I hear the thunder. I see the heron's screech before I hear it.

Light and sound, he said, are the stuff of all things. And the sound heard out at sea one night, a sound I didn't hear with my hearing, the sound that isn't a sound of two things striking together, that's the seed sound, the source sound of the sun and moon and the stars. The sun and the moon and the stars are condensations of that sound.

It wasn't what my father said that was important. It was the ageless silence of his voice that awakened something in me, a yearning in me.

After that I played only one other hurling match. Surrendering to a need for solitude and silence, I'd go off alone into the woods or into the hills, sitting all night in the crotch of a tree, sitting sometimes all day by a corrie lake in the mountains.

On a calm day in the mountains, I postponed all purpose and allowed my spirit to be still. When I was as calm as the lake was I mirrored the mountains as serenely as it did. Mirroring them, I didn't modify them. No ebbing into self-awareness shimmered them. Clear, like the lake, to my very depths, they touched the quick in me with their unperturbed, ageless summits. By nightfall there was no me. Where no perceiver was, where no organ of perception was, there was an eternal, serene perceiving.

Even tonight, overlaid. though they be by self-awareness and self-purpose, that corrie lake and that calm perceiving are within me. Within me, imperturbably in my depths, are the summits, are the elevations of spirit, I sometimes need. More often than not, I don't have access to them when I need them, but I know they are there.

All of this wasn't something I did. All of this, when I surrendered to them, was something my surroundings did for me. It was with my surroundings that I walked into myself and found eternity.

I walked back out of eternity happily able to settle for less.

But was it less?

Seen in a mood we have sometimes access to, the least, little thing is in no way less than the Supreme.

But I did settle for less. I settled for selfhood and ordinariness.

My capacity for ordinariness grew with the years. Ordinary work. Ordinary things. Ordinary people. Ordinary ways with things and with people.

So deeply presiding in me did this capacity for ordinariness become that one day, it occurred to me, it had grown into its opposite. I would sometimes experience a kind of rapturous incapacity to move on or away from the presence of some ordinary thing that had caught my attention.

Settling for less was a way to wonder.

Settling for less was a way to Connla's Well.

Connla and his well are within.

They are a mood, a way of seeing, that comes to the surface from within. And people who have found their way to that well, everything they say of it is true. It is an otherworldly well. That means it is a well of this, our ordinary world, when this, our ordinary world, is seen and perceived in that marvellous mood that emerges from within.

Growing in a shadowy cool arch, a hazel grows over it. All year round, but only now and then, a hazel nut falls onto it. Salmon who eat these nuts acquire the wisdom out of which all worlds are born. Returning downstream they carry it to the farthest reaches of the world's dreaming and waking.

And yes. It is true what they say: the rivers of Ireland have their source in this well.

And Connla? Who is he? He is you. He is me. At a depth of you, you are Connla.

At a depth of him also, my father was Connla. And, although I didn't know it, he wasn't only my natural father. In his ways and in his words, he was also my otherworldly father and, from the day I was born, I was in otherworldly fosterage to him. He nourished a way of seeing things in me. He nourished in me a way of being in the world.

When my father asked me how I was he didn't only mean how I was in this world, he was asking me how I was in all worlds. Was I the kind of person, he was asking, who would be welcome in all worlds? Were my feet philosophically fit to walk elsewhere?

And I knew what he meant: if you aren't philosophically fit to walk in the Otherworld you aren't philosophically fit to walk in this world. All other worlds and this world are one world. And the only philosophical words you need are wonder and wonder and again wonder.

As, at the end of their lives, some heroes of old sailed away in a crystal boat to the Otherworld so, at some depth of ourselves, did each of us come to this world, which we call ordinary, in a crystal boat.

There aren't many who know that these days, though. There aren't many who pass my house walking inland. There aren't many who know that the path to Connla's well is open. I know it.

As poet and philosopher, I walk the path to Connla's Well.

As poet and philosopher, it's my task to keep it open. (*Dreamtime*, pp. 192–5)

COMING OUT OF THE ANAESTHETIC
(Coming in to plenitude of being in the plenary world)

Talking with her recently, my niece Amanda reminded me that humanity has in the past been afflicted by some very destructive diseases, among them plague, pox and tuberculosis. The next big disease, she feared, will be madness.

In what sense madness? I enquired.

Madness in the sense of mental alienation from our deep mind and from how reality is, she replied.

Afterwards, sitting on alone, I wondered what she meant by our deep mind.

I remembered something Yeats said:

I know now that revelation is from the self, but from that age-long memoried self, that shapes the elaborate shell of the mollusc and the child in the womb, that teaches the birds to make their nests; and that genius is a crisis that joins that buried self for certain moments to our trivial daily mind.

I remembered something a remembering Inuit said:

In the very earliest time when both people and animals lived on earth a person could become an animal if he wanted to and an animal could become a human being. Sometimes they were people and sometimes animals, and there was no difference. All spoke the same language. That was the time when words were like magic. The human mind had mysterious powers. A word spoken by chance might have strange consequences. It would suddenly come alive and what people wanted to happen could happen all you had to do was say it. Nobody can explain this: that's the way it was.

It is of things as they now are that J.B.S. Haldane speaks when he says:

> It is my suspicion that the universe isn't only queerer than we suppose, it is queerer than we can suppose.

On the assumption that this is so, it must be good for us, it might even reconnect us with how reality is, were we to spend some time in Once-Upon-a-Time …

A shepherd he was, and always on May morning he would drive his sheep to higher grazing ground. No different this year than any previous year, he didn't need a dog to urge them on. As though they were glad to be free of the vexations of winter enclosure, they were lambs again, scampering and bounding upwards along old trails, up to new grass, up to what for them was their high home range.

Having nothing else to do, the shepherd sat on a turf covered rock, knitting a winter scarf for himself. Soon he saw a hare and then another hare. Finding each other, they stood on their hind legs and sniffed each other. The better to see them, the shepherd leaned so steeply aside that his ball of thread rolled off his lap, down the hillside. Gone down to retrieve it, he saw to his utter surprise that it had disappeared through a great opening in the hill. For fifty years he had come to this hill, spending all summer long up here, he knew it as well as he knew his own yard, and yet he had never caught sight of this opening. Had it just happened? Or was it that, normally closed to us, reality was now, for its own good reasons, opening up to us? If it was, he wouldn't be found wanting. He walked through and found himself in a great cavern. As though illumined by a light from within himself, he saw a royal, crowned figure lying asleep on an oak bed. How he didn't know, but he knew it was King Arthur. Arthur it was. Bright as his legend. Bright as our memory of him.

Beside the oak bed there was an oak table. On it there was a horn and a sword. Picking it up, he crashed the sword down on the table, making a sound much louder than he expected.

King Arthur awoke, lifted his head off the pillow, turned toward him and said, had you picked up the trumpet and blown it I The Once and Future King would have shaken off sleep, would have risen up and returned among people, the marvellous world as it used to be returning with me. Now I return to sleep. For centuries maybe. For longer maybe. Till someone finds the opening.

Disappointed and alarmed, the shepherd backed away, picking up his ball of thread as he did so. Back in the customary world he looked round, but, as though it had never been, there was now no opening in reality.

And so we ask, what has happened to Arthur in us? What has happened to what is right royal in us? What has happened to what is regal in us? What has happened to what is sovereign in us?

Peter: Did you see an old woman going down the path?
Patrick: I did not, but I saw a young girl, and she had the walk of a queen.

When and how did we lose that walk? How and when will we regain it?

I think of three horn calls: the horn call that will awaken Arthur and his world in us, the horn call that will awaken Morgan La Faye and her world in us, the horn call that will awaken Merlin and his world in us.
Arthur we can be.
Morgan La Faye we can be.
And Merlin, sage of the woods who sometimes comes among us speaking the twelve languages of the wind and the eighteen languages of the rain, him we can be.
Whoever you are, that's who you are, a young woman with the walk of a queen.

*** *** ***

> I went out to the hazel wood,
> Because a fire was in my head,
> And cut and peeled a hazel wand,
> And hooked a berry to a thread;
> And when white moths were on the wing
> And moth-like stars were flickering out,
> I dropped the berry in the stream
> And caught a little silver trout.
>
> When I had laid it on the floor
> I went to blow the fire aflame,
> But something rustled on the floor,

And someone called me by my name:
It had become a glimmering girl
With apple blossom in her hair
Who called me by my name and ran
And faded through the brightening air.

Though I am old with wandering
Through hollow lands and hilly lands.
I will find out where she has gone
And kiss her lips and take her hands;
And walk among long dappled grass,
And pluck till time and times are done
The silver apples of the moon,
The golden apples of the sun.

***   ***   ***

He was an inshore fisherman. He picked mussels and limpets and periwinkles from the rocks. He dug in the tidal sands for razor fish and cockles. As though led to them by a sixth sense, he harvested oysters and clams. And, rowing himself up and down the inlets, he fished with nets for shrimp when they were in season. Once, during an autumn spring-tide the wind was blowing from the land and when it did ebb the sea retreated farther than he had ever seen, out beyond three sea stacks. leaving only a shallow channel, loud with waders, in between. Greedily anticipating the rich pickings he would find, he crossed the channel, the birds taking affrighted flight, and he set to work. So absorbed did he become filling bag after bag, first with mussels and then with winkles, that he lost all sense of time and when, the last bag full, he looked up, he saw that the tide had turned and had cut him off. Having learned the hard way that he had no chance against currents so continuously swirling, he decided there was nothing for it but to sit it out until the next ebbtide.

Making his way to it, he sat in the lee of a great ledge of rock. Night came down. At the full coming up and then rising high in the sky, the moon was so bright it was almost like day. In the small hours he got up to work a stiffness and chill out of his body, out of his mind as well, and it was then he saw them, seals coming ashore, and the wonder of it was that, having struggled up onto the rock ledges, they dropped their seal coats and became human beings. Never had he seen their like for beauty, but what was yet more marvellous, they continually flourished in the wonder of each other. He watched them, entranced by them, till dawn. Till ebbtide. And then, like he was dreaming, like he was doing it in a dream, all thought of shellfish forgotten, he stole around, picked up one of the seal coats and started for home, walking hip deep across the channel.

Since, without her coat, the sealwoman couldn't turn back into a seal and swim away as all the others were now doing, she followed him, across the channel, up the shore, along the small roads, into his house. That night, after she had fallen asleep, he left their bed and went out and, leaning a ladder against it, he hid the seal coat in the thatch.

In time a child was born to them. And then another. And another.

Often, during those years, she would go down to the shore and while she was there, looking seaward, you might as well not talk to her at all or call her, for she wouldn't hear you.

One day, as she was kneading dough at a great board table, a drop of seal oil fell down into it. Getting the smell of it, it all came back to her, her life as a seal in the sea, her sons and her daughters in the sea, her grandmothers in the sea. Aching, knowingly now, to be with them, she crossed the yard to an outhouse, came back with a ladder, leaned it against the thatch, dug in it, and found her seal coat. Reaching the lip of the tide, she draped it over her shoulders, she became a seal, and was gone. Not forever though, for some mornings, looking at each other, her children on land will see that their hair has been combed in the night, her way of telling them that she has been back, and will come back.

With good reason, some of us settle for a little life. Never do we cross a channel at ebbtide. Never do we run the risk of being cut off from an acquired but fixed sense of who we are. Never, coming up out of our culture, do we drop our conditioning, all of it, leaving it behind us, unregarded, on the rocks. Sometimes it happens though. A drop of seal oil falls down into our fixed sense of ourselves and 'tis as if a spell has been broken.

Where we tend to see fixity the story sees fluency and the day will surely come when we will be happy to flow, not just from one to another identity but from identity as such, back into God.

*** *** ***

Tegid Foel and Ceridwen were wed. A year later in a house that looked like a folktale had imagined it a daughter was born to them. Then a son. The son was as ugly as the daughter was fair. Hardly had they washed him and dried him than they called him Morfran, meaning Great Crow. Worse still. He grew every year more ugly and now, so as not to lie about him, they called him Afagdhu, meaning Utter Darkness. But Ceridwen, a nature goddess in disguise, so some thought no, she was determined that her son would not be an outcast because of his ugliness. She would make him all-wise, and this, his wisdom, would ensure that he would be welcome at the tables of chieftains in their ringforts and of kings in their high, never to be conquered castles.

A cauldron Ceridwen had, and now, as at its making, she chanted a variety of spells, long and short, all of them in an unknown language, into it, all round inside it, all round outside it, into its rim. Herbs boiling water wouldn't boil these spells would boil, compelling them to yield up their most secret essences.

Intending to brew a drop of wisdom for Afagdhu, for him alone, Ceridwen charged Mordha, an elderly man, to procure the logs, and Gwion Back, a boy, him she charged to tend the fire, and this they must do every day for a year and a day. Also, every day for a year and a day, Ceridwen would herself go out into the world seeking the necessary herbs, some of them rare, some of them growing so briefly in places so occult that only someone with second sight would find them.

Things went well.

Sometimes in the night Ceridwen would dream of a herb and off she would go in the morning, her dream having shown her the way.

That's how it was, day after day, Mordha bringing in the logs, Gwion Back tending the ever fervent fire, Ceridwen coming home with the herbs, the cauldron boiling, not boiling itself away, not steaming away, everything kept within, a spell she had spoken having ensured this.

On the last night of the long wait Ceridwen dreamed of yet one more herb growing in an old heron's nest at the top of the tree in a wood far away. Determined to be home early, she set out early.

At the time she expected to be back but wasn't yet back there was thunder in the cauldron. Contained within the cauldron, it was thunder more thunderous than was ever heard among the open mountains. Then there was silence. Still terrified, neither Mordha nor Gwion Back reached in to collect the brewed drop of wisdom. Now again there was thunder, this time snarling, and angry, and as though it had been spat out, out over the rim of the cauldron came the drop of wisdom. It landed on Gwion Back's thumb. It burned him, he licked it and, instantly now, he was all wise, all knowing, all seeing, seeing endlessly into the past, endlessly into the present, endlessly into the future. What had been meant for Afagdhu, was his by accident. Imagining Ceridwen's wrath, he rushed out of doors, only just in time, for with a scream the cauldron burst, its boiling contents burning a path for itself down the hillside into the river below Gwyddno Faranhir's salmon weir. Downstream from there Gwyddno's horses came to drink and, too much for them, the power in the water killed them.

Soon Ceridwen was coming over the brow of the hill. Seeing the still steaming path down to the river, she guessed what had happened and now, as the bursting cauldron had screamed, she screamed. Gwion Back took to flight. Her wrath scorching herself and the grass under her feet, she set off in pursuit. Just as she was about to lay vengeful hands on him, he became a hare. Not to be outdone, she became a hound. Again, just as she was about to close her mouth on him he leaped and became a salmon in the river. Instantly, she was an otter chasing him down. Rising up, he became a bird of the air but there she was, a falcon bearing down on him. Overflying a farm yard with great heaps of winnowed wheat in it, he dropped down, a grain among millions. A match for him whatever he did, she plunged and, shedding her falcon form, there she was, a red-combed black hen eyeing the wheat grains, swallowing the one with a difference.

The bother was, back to herself in her house, she knew she was pregnant with him. She pregnant with defeat. With defeat for herself. With defeat for Afagdhu. And nine months to wait until, she could lay hands on him. He taking from her, digesting her. He kicking her. No. Na now.

Not now. Now, for now, she wasn't a match for him. And one thing she knew: he would go to full term.

Three weeks overdue, she screamed him out into her waiting hands, but no, defeated by him still, she couldn't do it, she couldn't kill him.

Within hours, her strength returned to her, she stitched him into a leather satchel, she walked west to the sea and committed him, to her surprise with prayers, to an outgoing tide. Out, out, out he was carried. Out beyond view. Her anger more hurtful because more useless, she turned for home.

Days and years ran on. It was May morning and always on May morning there would be a first run of salmon in off the sea and up the river, tidal at first and then cascading.

Busy with more urgent tasks himself, Gwyddno asked Ellflin, his not so clever son, to go down to the weir and bag the netted salmon.

To Ellflin's dismay, there were no salmon and, turning for home, he could well imagine how angry his father would be when he gave him the news, and worse, known for his stupidity, he as he always was would be to blame. Dreading the encounter, he looked back in the hopeless hope that he might see a gleam of silver ascending the river. What he saw instead was a gleaming something hanging from the near weir pole. Intrigued, in a childlike way, he retraced his steps, the fully risen but still low sun picking out the marvel, whatever it might be. Afraid at first to touch it, it frightened him all the more when he figured that it was a satchel encrusted all over with barnacles and mussels and little flutterings of seaweed. Eventually, in the hope that he'd find something in it that would pacify his father, he lifted it off, down onto the deck, he unstitched it and, looking down into it, he saw a bright-browed wonder child, saw him and heard him, he singing poems, their words more real than the things they talked about, hawks and mountain havens, salmon and stars.

Now called Bright Brow, now called Taliesin, Gwion Back sings. Still in the satchel he sings:

> There is news of the macrocosm in us its microcosm.
> The richer we are in ourselves the richer our sense
> of the universe.
> What we come home to in ourselves we come home to
> in the universe.
> When we come home to soul in ourselves we come
>   home to soul in the universe.

Walking away, and growing to full human height, he sings:

> Purpose in perceiving perverts perceiving. Self-will in perceiving perverts perceiving. A perceiver in perceiving perverts perceiving.

> Perceiving.

Perceiving these mountains.

Perceiving them beyond the wound of someone perceiving and something perceived.

Perceiving is.

Perceiving these mountains in the unwounded

Oneness of God ...

It is a question that many adults in our culture might ask: what has happened to the wonder child in us?

And how come our culture didn't do for us what Ceridwen did for Gwion Back?

How come that it didn't stitch us into a second womb or cocoon and return us into the genius of the universe.

The universe in which a caterpillar becomes a butterfly.

The universe in which Gwion Back becomes a wonder child.

The universe which, for all we know, might already have spun a cocoon for itself.

It is what the story would teach us: better to trust the genius of the universe in us than to trust our trivial daily minds.

*** *** ***

Moments there are.

There is the moment when we see something otherwise quite ordinary, such as smoke from our chimney, and we know, seeing it, that the universe is stranger, maybe queerer, than we can suppose.

The moment when reality opens or maybe it is our mind that opens, there being days when mind and reality are one and the same.

The moment when, hearing our name called, our census-form sense of ourselves falls from us.

The moment when a drop of seal oil falls down into our world and we know that our empirical experience of ourselves, whether as seal, woman or whatever, isn't the whole story.

The moment when we come upon the wonder child we might have been or, starting again, could yet be, becoming in time the great remembered bard of a people.

I think of it, the day when Orion stands at our door. Like a postman, he returns to us everything we have said about the universe.

Seeing how dumbfounded we are, he tells us that no, the universe doesn't recognise itself in what we say about it.

Observing our continuing perplexity he says, partial knowledge is nescience, and that is as true of our partial knowledge of ourselves as it is of our partial knowledge of the universe.

I think of it, the day when Prospero buried his book,
I think of it, the day when, just for the day,

> Francis Bacon buries his book called Novum Organum.
> Galileo Galilei buries his book called Siderius Nuncius.
> Isaac Newton buries his book called Principia Mathematica.
> Albert Einstein buries his book called The General Theory of Relativity.

Day when, night when, the universe shines thoroughly through the impairments of our thinking about it.

Day when, coming home, the Mental Traveller looks up and sees smoke rising from his chimney. After incarnations of seeking, sometimes hunting, he has found the place and the state of mind to set out from.

One day, yearning beyond Paradise, we will resist the call and the lure of the girl with apple blossom in her hair. And then, the trail he has given his name to descending beneath us, we will run the risk of honouring our purposed but wisely postponed rendezvous with Bright Angel. (*Slí na Fírinne*, pp. 48, 50–9)

An Illumination: Coda

Seán Aherne

On the first anniversary of John Moriarty's death I was in his house at 3.30 pm with others. I touched his big chair as one would touch a relic. I missed the huge presence that used to sit there welcoming me. I glanced at the stack of some 3000 pages beside his chair. I asked John to guide me to a page he wanted me to read. Then I put my hand into the paper stack about one tenth down and took out a large white page with just one line at top: 'In Paradise the Physics of Atoms is the Physics of Lauds.'

I was amazed at the terseness of it and muttered to myself: 'It will take me some time to figure this one out.' Then I focused on the first words, 'In Paradise', and it hit me. That's where John is speaking from now! That's his main address. He is right, he is praising.

I put the page back in the pile.

All evening I marvelled at that line and before sleeping at 1.20 am I asked John to explain it to me as I slept.

Next morning I awoke at 7.20 am and I felt John speaking through me and I wrote:

> In Paradise the physics of atoms is (gives way to) the physics of Lauds.
> This is from my new address
> I am in Paradise now
> The mortal coil is thrown off
> No need to worry about my body
> I don't need it more
> The physics of atoms is gone
> Here all is Praise and thanks
> Everlasting hymns of Praise to God I am
> The Kedusah I am now
> The Trishagion I am now
> The Sanctus I am now
> *Is naofacht mé anois*
> I am one in the ONE
> I am back in the Vastness of God which I never left
> I have Paradisal Perception
> I have the Vision that sustains
> Eye hath not seen, nor ear heard what I am now enjoying
> I have come home singing
> I have come home rejoicing
> Laudate, gaudete
> *Canaigi amhráin molta*

Tógaigí gártha áthais
Bíodh Lúchair oraidh
Táim ar Shlí na Fírrine
Agus is iontach e
Agus is iontas e
On the voyage of my immortality
Here all is Praise and Thanks to the One who dreamed me
And by whom I was dreamed
I wouldn't change it for the world
So Eileen don't be sad for me
When the time is right I'll be waiting for you with open arms
and lead you safely home
And hold you close again forever
Here the sun never sets
Here it is always light
Here it is perpetual Day
A Day that never ends
A Day continually unfolding
A Day to go more and more into the very depths of reality
A Day to grow in fuller appreciation of the Mystery of Divine Ground
Juliana was right when she said All shall be well
And all manner of things shall be well for it is so
The end of craving I have attained
Nothing else do I seek
So rejoice and praise with me today

Moladh go deo le Dia mor na gloire
Mile gloir do Dhia
Gloir do Dhia
Mile gloir do Dhia Naofa.
Amen. Amen.
    John Moriarty
    Paradise Regained.

Notes

1. Edna O'Brien, *The Little Red Chairs* (New York 2015), p. 15.
2. Ibid. p. 20.
3. Private correspondence with Brendan O'Donoghue, 12 January 2016.
4. Aidan Mathews, 'Turtle Was Gone a Long Time (Volume 1: Crossing the Kedron)', *The Furrow* 1998.
5. Brendan O'Donoghue (ed.), *A Moriarty Reader: Preparing for Early Spring* (Dublin 2013), p. 252.
6. Ibid.
7. Ibid., p. 280.
8. Ibid., pp. 280–1.
9. Ibid., p. 288.
10. Ibid., p. 303.
11. Ibid., p. 290.
12. Ibid., p. 294.
13. Ibid., p. 297.
14. Ibid., p. 302.
15. Ibid., p. 308.
16. Ibid., p. 309.
17. Ibid., p. 312.
18. Ibid., p. 316.
19. Ibid., p. 317.
20. Ibid., p. 318.
21. Ibid., p. 321.
22. Ibid., p. 328.
23. John Moriarty, *Slí na Fírinne* (Dublin 2006), p. 26.
24. Ibid.
25. Ibid., p. 127.
26. Ibid., p. 21.
27. Jerry White, 'Figure of Speech: How language constitutes human consciousness,' *Literary Review of Canada,* July/August, 2016, p. 7.
28. John Moriarty, *Nostos: An Autobiography* (Dublin 2001), p. 21.

John Moriarty Publications and Related Works

For the Lilliput Press, Dublin:

Dreamtime (1994, 1999)
Turtle Was Gone a Long Time:
  Crossing the Kedron (Volume 1, 1996)
  Horsehead Nebula Neighing (Volume 2, 1997)
  Anaconda Canoe (Volume 3, 1998)
Nostos, An Autobiography (2001)
Invoking Ireland (2005)
Night Journey to Budd Gaia (2006)
What the Curlew Said, Nostos Continued (2007)
Serious Sounds (2007)
One Evening in Eden (2007) (boxed CD collection of talks, stories and poetry)

Brendan O'Donoghue (ed.), *A Moriarty Reader, Preparing for Early Spring* (2013)
Mary McGillicuddy, *John Moriarty: Not the Whole Story* (2018)

For Slí na Fírinne Publishing, Kerry:

Slí na Fírinne (2006)
Urbi et Orbi (2006)